appliqué
class

ISBN 978-0-470-88719-6

Printed in China

10 9 8 7 6 5 4 3 2 1

Our Promise
Prior to publication we cut, sew, and assemble at least four blocks of every quilt to verify the accuracy of our patterns and instructions. Then an experienced team of editors reviews the materials lists, how-to directions, and illustrations to make sure the information we provide you is clear, concise, and complete.

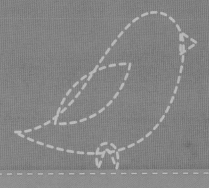

Better Homes and Gardens®

appliqué
class

20 Favorite Projects
from the Editors of *American
Patchwork & Quilting*®

WILEY

John Wiley & Sons, Inc.

contents

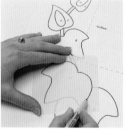

appliqué primer

easy

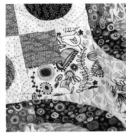

intermediate

advanced

etc.

ap·pli·qué

"A decoration or trimming made of one material attached by sewing, gluing, etc. to another."

—WEBSTER'S NEW WORLD COLLEGE DICTIONARY, 4TH EDITION

While the definition above is accurate, the word "appliqué" takes on a greater meaning in the quilting world. It's not only the decoration that's attached to fabric, it's a technique that allows quilters to give their projects a personal touch. Beyond the straight cuts made by a rotary cutter and the machine-sewn lines of a pieced quilt, appliqué allows quilters the liberty to embellish their projects with interesting shapes. A traditional quilt, made by sewing blocks together in rows, is beautiful in its own right with its play on color, hue, and shape. But add appliqué cutouts, such as flowers, leaves, circles, or vines, and suddenly the quilt gains a certain "wow" factor, making it an object to admire with its graceful curves, layered pieces, and elegant shapes.

While the art of appliqué is not a new one, many methods for preparing, positioning, and attaching the appliqué pieces have evolved over the years, which perhaps has led many to hesitate trying the technique. If you're an admirer of appliqué and have yet to take the plunge into the craft, the pages of the Appliqué Primer that follow will help get you on your way.

When starting out in appliqué, the main thing to keep in mind is that there is more than one way to achieve similar results. For example, when preparing appliqué shapes, one person may prefer to baste the raw edges of the shapes, while another may find using freezer-paper templates to be a more enjoyable method. Still another person might prefer the spray-starch method, and yet another may choose a slightly different freezer-paper technique. But in the end, all of these methods are just different options for turning under the seam allowances of your appliqué shapes. Each one will result in a slightly different look, so it's up to you to determine your preferred method.

Beyond the pages of the Appliqué Primer, you'll discover three sections of appliqué projects, divided into "Easy," "Intermediate," and "Advanced" sections. Within the instructions for each project, you'll find that the designers used their own preferred techniques. You needn't feel limited to this way. If you wish, feel free to modify the instructions using the methods found in the Primer. Just keep in mind the end result you want to accomplish. For instance, a project using fusible web in the instructions will require that you add seam allowances to the patterns if you'd rather use a freezer-paper method for preparing the pieces instead.

Wherever your current appliqué skills are, we hope you'll find this book a helpful resource to add to your quilting library, and a useful tool for taking your skills to the next level.

Enjoy!

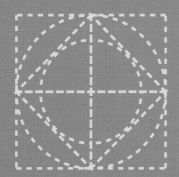

appliqué primer

Whether you're new to appliqué, want to further your skills, or simply need a go-to reference, turn to this step-by-step guide to help you as you work on all your appliqué projects.

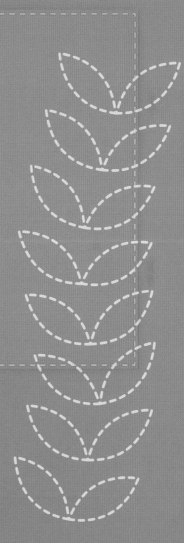

templates

An appliqué template is a pattern used to trace the appliqué shape onto fabric. The template's material depends on how often the template will be used. Make sure that your template will hold up to the wear that it receives from multiple tracings without deteriorating at the edges. A sturdy, durable material such as template plastic, available at quilt and crafts supply stores, is suitable for making permanent templates for scissors-cut appliqué pieces.

making appliqué templates

[1] For most appliqué techniques you need to make your templates the exact size of the finished pieces with no seam allowances included. The seam allowances are added when you cut out the appliqué pieces. Trace the patterns onto template plastic using a permanent marker. Use a ruler for any straight lines (see **Photo 1**).

[2] Mark each appliqué template with its letter designation, grain line (if indicated), block name, and appliqué sequence order. (See *page 11* for more information on Stitching Sequence.) Mark an X on edges that do not need to be turned under and transfer the Xs to the fabric shapes when you trace around the templates (see **Photo 2**).

[3] Cut out each template, then verify their accuracy by placing them over their printed patterns (see **Photo 3**).

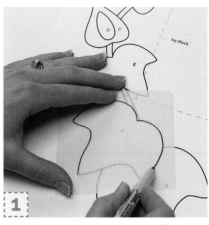

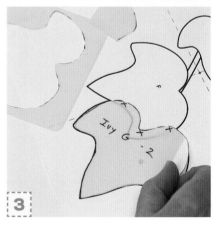

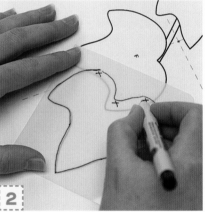

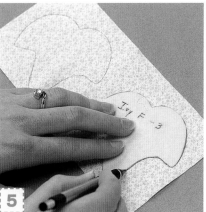
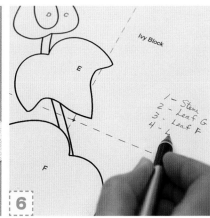

using appliqué templates

[1] Choose a marking tool to trace around the templates on fabric. A pencil works well on light-color fabric; a white, silver, or yellow dressmaker's pencil is a good choice on dark-color fabric. If you're using a pencil, keep the point sharp to ensure accuracy. Do not use a ballpoint or ink pen; it may bleed when washed. Test all marking tools on a fabric scrap before using them (see **Photo 4**).

[2] Place templates on the fabric, positioning them at least ½" apart. (Whether you place them faceup or facedown on the fabric's right or wrong side depends on the appliqué method you choose.) Trace around each template with your selected marking tool. The drawn lines represent the sewing lines. The specific appliqué technique you choose will dictate how much, if any, seam allowance you leave when cutting out the shape (see **Photo 5**).

[3] Cut out the appliqué shapes, including seam allowances if necessary for your chosen appliqué method.

stitching sequence

[1] Edges of appliqué pieces that will be covered by other pieces do not need to be turned under before they are appliquéd. By preparing all your appliqué pieces at one time, you can plan any overlaps, which will save stitching time and considerable bulk in the finished project.

[2] If your pattern does not indicate a numerical stitching sequence, observe which piece is closest to the foundation fabric and farthest away from you. That is the first piece you should appliqué to the foundation. Appliqué the rest of the pieces to the foundation, working from the bottom layer to the top (see **Photo 6**).

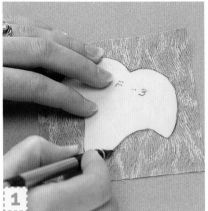

preparing appliqué pieces

Prepare your appliqué pieces according to the needs of your chosen appliqué method. Preparation options include basting, freezer paper, spray starch, and fusible web. Read the introduction to each method that follows to determine which one will work for your selected method.

basting method

This method uses a reusable template, marking tool, and thread to prepare appliqué pieces for hand or machine appliqué.

[1] Place your templates on the right side of the fabric, positioning them at least ½" apart; trace. (see **Photo 1**).

[2] Cut out the appliqué shapes, adding a ³⁄₁₆" seam allowance to all edges. Clip inside curves and points to within a thread of the marked lines, making clips closer together in the curved areas. Try to make your clips on the bias grain of the seam allowance, which means your clips will be often diagonal, rather than perpendicular, lines. This directional clipping prevents fabric from raveling while you're working with the edges (see **Photo 2**). **Note:** Some hand quilters who use the needle-turn appliqué method choose to stop their appliqué preparation with this step (for more information, see Needle-Turn Appliqué, on *page 28*).

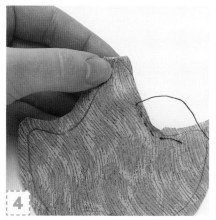 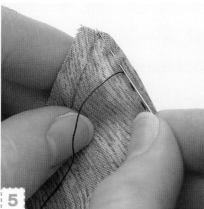 

[3] Working from the right side of the appliqué piece and beginning at an inner point, use a contrasting color thread to baste the seam allowance under following the marked lines. For easier removal of the thread later, begin and end your basting thread on the right side of the appliqué piece (see **Photo 3**).

[4] For a sharp outer point, fold the fabric straight over the point (see **Photo 4**).

[5] Then fold in an adjacent seam allowance, overlapping the folded point. Baste in place (see **Photo 5**).

[6] As you reach the outer point, fold over the remaining adjacent seam allowance and continue basting around the shape (see **Photo 6**).

freezer-paper wrong-side method 1

This method uses freezer-paper templates to hold the seam allowances of the appliqué pieces in place. This technique may be used to prepare pieces for hand or machine appliqué.

[1] Trace the appliqué patterns on the dull side of the freezer paper. Cut out the shapes on the traced lines to make freezer-paper templates (see **Photo 1**).

[2] Place the freezer-paper templates dull side up on the right side of the fabric. While holding the freezer paper in place, cut the shapes from the fabric, adding a ³⁄₁₆" seam allowance to all edges (see **Photo 2**).

[3] Turn the freezer-paper templates shiny side up and place on the wrong side of the appliqué shape. Clip the inside curves or points on the appliqué shapes (see **Photo 3**). When clipping inside curves, clip halfway through the seam allowances. Try to make your clips on the bias grain of the seam allowance, which means your clips often will be diagonal, rather than perpendicular, lines. This directional clipping prevents fabric from raveling while you're working with the edges (see **Photo 4**).

[4] Beginning at an inner point of an appliqué shape, use the tip of a hot, dry iron to push the seam allowance over the edge of the freezer paper. The seam allowance will adhere to the shiny side of the freezer paper. **Note:** Do not touch the iron soleplate to the freezer paper past the turned fabric edge (see **Photo 5**).

[5] Continue working around the appliqué shape, turning one small area at a time and pressing the seam allowance up and over the freezer paper (see **Photo 5**). Make certain the appliqué fabric is pressed taut against the freezer-paper template.

Small pleats in the fabric may appear as you round outer curves. If there is too much bulk in a seam allowance, make small V clips around outer curves to ease the fabric around the edge (see **Photo 6**).

[6] For a sharp outer point, fold the fabric straight over the point of the freezer-paper template; press to freezer paper (see **Photo 7**).

[7] With the tip of the iron, push an adjacent seam allowance over the edge of the freezer paper (see **Photo 8**).

[8] Repeat with the remaining adjacent seam allowance, pushing the seam allowance taut to ensure a sharp point.

tip

Removing a freezer-paper template after an appliqué shape has been stitched in place can be done in a couple of ways.

- You may stitch the appliquéd shape to the foundation, leaving a small opening to pull out the template. Use the tip of your needle to loosen the freezer-paper template. Pull the template out through the opening and stitch the opening closed.
- You may stitch the entire appliqué shape in place. From the wrong side, carefully snip through the appliqué foundation only. Remove the template through the opening, then stitch the opening closed.

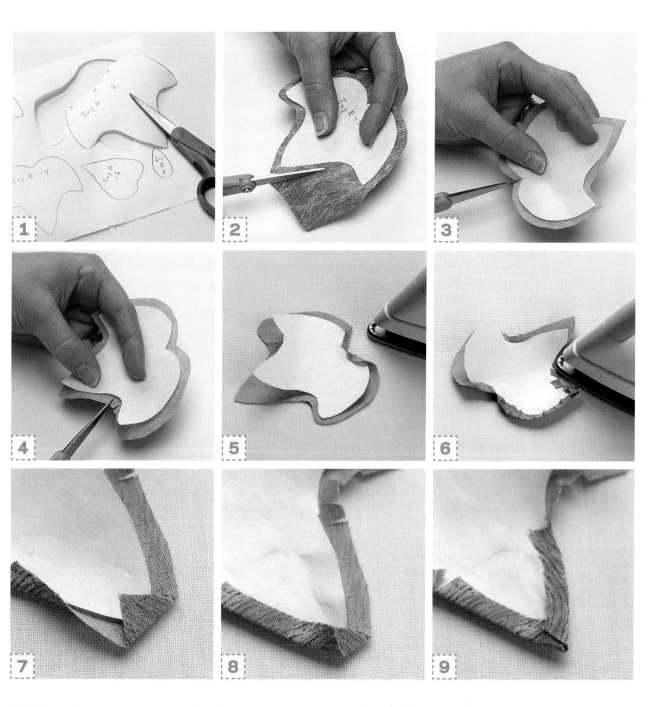

[9] After all edges are pressed, let the appliqué shape cool, then either remove the freezer-paper template before proceeding with the desired hand- or machine-appliqué technique or leave in to stitch (see **Photo 9**). (See tip box, *opposite*, for information on removing templates after appliqué has been sewn in place.)

freezer-paper wrong-side method 2

This technique involves pressing entire freezer-paper templates, shiny side down, to the appliqué fabric. The freezer paper is removed before the appliqué is sewn in place. (Refer to Using Freezer Paper, *opposite*, for additional information.) This technique may be used to prepare pieces for hand or machine appliqué.

[1] Trace a reverse image of the appliqué patterns on the dull side of the freezer paper (see **Photo 1**). Cut out the shapes on the traced lines to make freezer-paper templates. **Note:** To create a reverse image, tape the appliqué pattern facedown on a light box or sunny window (see tip box, *below*).

[2] Place the appliqué fabric wrong side up on a pressing surface. With a dry iron on a cotton setting, press a freezer-paper shape, shiny side down, to the appliqué fabric. Leave the iron on the paper for a few seconds. Lift the iron to check that the template is completely adhered to the fabric (see **Photo 2**). If the template is not completely adhered, press again.

[3] Cut out the appliqué shape, adding a $\frac{3}{16}$" seam allowance to all edges. Clip inside curves or points on the appliqué shape (see **Photo 3**). When clipping inside curves, clip halfway through seam allowance (see **Photo 4**). Try to make your clips on the bias grain of the seam allowance, which means clips often will be on diagonal, rather than perpendicular, lines. This directional clipping prevents fabric from raveling while you're working with the edges.

[4] Beginning at one inner point of an appliqué shape, use the tip of a dry, hot iron to push the seam allowance over the edge of the freezer paper to create a sharp edge (see **Photo 5**). **Note:** The seam allowance will not adhere to the dull side of the freezer paper.

[5] Continue working around the appliqué shape, turning one small area at a time and pressing the seam allowance up and over the freezer paper. Make certain the appliqué fabric is pressed taut against the edges of the freezer-paper template (see **Photo 6**).

Small pleats in the fabric may appear as you round outer curves. If there is too much bulk in a seam allowance, make small V clips around outer curves to ease the fabric around the edge.

[6] For a sharp outer point, fold the fabric straight over the point of the freezer-paper template; press.

tip

Some appliqué techniques require you to make a reverse image of the shapes. To do so, tape the appliqué pattern facedown on a light box or sunny window. Secure a piece of tracing paper over the shape and trace with a fine-line marker or mechanical pencil.

Mark its name or number and the word "reversed" on the traced pattern. This will serve as a reminder when you're using the shape that you've already reversed the image.

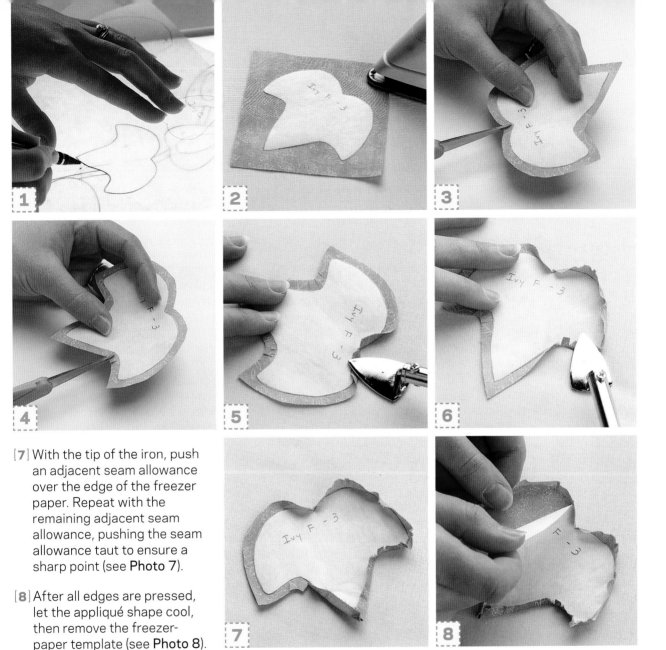

[7] With the tip of the iron, push an adjacent seam allowance over the edge of the freezer paper. Repeat with the remaining adjacent seam allowance, pushing the seam allowance taut to ensure a sharp point (see **Photo 7**).

[8] After all edges are pressed, let the appliqué shape cool, then remove the freezer-paper template (see **Photo 8**).

USING FREEZER PAPER
Many quilters choose to use freezer paper for appliqué. Available in grocery stores and some quilt shops, freezer paper has a shiny coating on one side that temporarily adheres to fabric when pressed with a warm iron. It is not necessary to consider the grain line of the fabric when utilizing freezer-paper templates.

spray-starch method

With this method, spray starch holds the appliqué's seam allowances against a reusable, heat-resistant template, which is removed before the appliqué is sewn in place. This technique may be used to prepare pieces for hand or machine appliqué.

[1] Make a heat-resistant plastic template the exact finished size of the appliqué motif (see **Photo 1**). Mark the template's right side.

[2] Place the template wrong side up on the wrong side of the appliqué fabric and trace. Cut around the shape, adding a ³⁄₁₆" seam allowance to all edges (see **Photo 2**).

[3] With wrong sides up, center the template on the appliqué fabric shape. Spray a small amount of starch into a dish. Working on a pressing surface covered with a tea towel or muslin, dip a cotton swab in the starch and moisten the outer edge of the seam allowance (see **Photo 3**).

[4] Clip all inside points. Beginning at an inside point, use the tip of a hot, dry iron to turn the seam allowance over the edge of the template and press it in place until the fabric is dry (see **Photo 4**).

[5] Continue pressing around the appliqué shape, clipping inside curves or points and adding starch as necessary (see **Photo 5**). When clipping inside curves, clip halfway through the seam allowance. Try to make your clips on the bias grain of the seam allowance, which means your clips often will be diagonal, rather than perpendicular, lines. This directional clipping prevents fabric from raveling while you're working with the edges. Make certain the fabric is pressed taut against the appliqué template.

[6] To make a sharp outer point, moisten the seam allowance and fold the fabric point straight over the point of the plastic template. Push one adjacent edge of the seam allowance over the edge of the template. Repeat with the remaining adjacent seam allowance (see **Photo 6**).

Small pleats in the fabric may appear as you round outer curves. If there is too much bulk in the seam allowance, make small V clips around outer curves to ease the fabric around the edge.

[7] Press the appliqué from the right side (see **Photo 7**), then remove the template (see **Photo 8**).

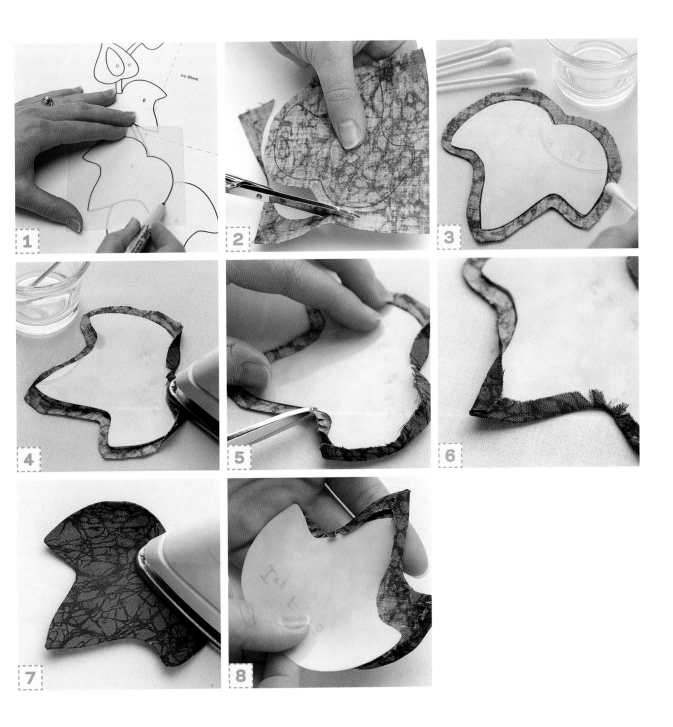

freezer-paper right-side method

This technique involves pressing the shiny side of the freezer-paper templates to the right side of the appliqué fabric. The seam allowances are not turned under. (Refer to Using Freezer Paper on *page 17* for additional information.) This technique may be used to prepare pieces for needle-turn appliqué (see *page 28*).

[1] Trace finished-size appliqué patterns onto the dull side of the freezer paper (see **Photo 1**). Cut out the shapes on the traced lines to make freezer-paper templates.

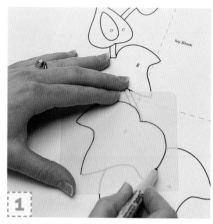

[2] Place the appliqué fabric right side up on a pressing surface. With a dry iron on a cotton setting, press a freezer-paper template, shiny side down, to the appliqué fabric (see **Photo 2**). Leave the iron on the paper for a few seconds. Lift the iron to check that the template is completely adhered to the fabric. If the template is not completely adhered, press again.

[3] Cut out the appliqué shape, adding a 3⁄16" seam allowance to all edges. Clip inside curves or points on the appliqué shape. When clipping inside curves, clip halfway through seam allowance (see **Photo 3**). Try to make your clips on the bias grain of the seam allowance, which means your clips will be diagonal, rather than perpendicular, lines. This directional clipping prevents fabric from raveling while you're working with the edges.

[4] Do not remove the template until the appliqué piece is stitched in place.

fusible-web method

This method eliminates the need to turn under any seam allowances. Choose a lightweight, paper-backed fusible web that can be stitched through unless you plan to leave the appliqué edges unfinished. If the appliqué edges will not be sewn in place, you may wish to use a heavyweight, no-sew fusible web. This technique is commonly used for machine appliqué, but also can be used for hand appliqué.

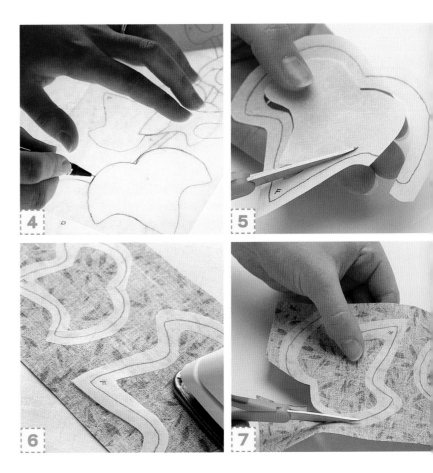

1] Position the fusible web with the paper side up over the appliqué patterns and place on light box. Use a pencil to trace each pattern the specified number of times (see **Photo 4**). If you are tracing multiple pieces at one time, leave at least ½" between tracings. **Note:** If you are not using an appliqué pattern designed especially for fusible web, you will need to create a mirror image of the pattern before tracing it. If you don't, your appliqués will be reversed once you cut them from fabric. To create a reverse image, tape the appliqué pattern facedown on a light box or sunny window (see tip box on *page 16*).

   Cut out the traced appliqué patterns roughly ¼" outside the traced lines. Do not cut directly on the traced lines.

2] If you are working with multiple appliqué layers or want to reduce the stiffness of the finished project, consider cutting away the center of your fusible web shapes. To do this, cut ¼" inside the traced lines and discard the centers (see **Photo 5**).

[3] Place the fusible-web shapes paper side up on the back of the designated appliqué fabrics. Press in place following the manufacturer's instructions (see **Photo 6**). Do not slide the iron, but pick it up to move it from one area to the next. Let the appliqué shapes cool.

[4] Cut out the fabric shapes on the drawn lines (see **Photo 7**). Peel off the paper backings.

positioning appliqué pieces

There are many ways to position pieces for appliqué. Some require more preparation than others. If you're new to appliqué, experiment with different positioning methods to select the one that's best for you.

folded-foundation method

[1] Cut the appliqué foundation fabric larger than the desired finished size to allow for any take-up in the fabric that might occur during the appliqué process. For example, for a 12" finished square, cut a 14"-square appliqué foundation. When the appliqué is complete, you'll trim the foundation to 12½" square. (The extra ¼" on each side will be used for seam allowances when assembling the quilt top.)

[2] Fold the square appliqué foundation in half vertically and horizontally to find the center and divide the square into quarters. Lightly finger-press to create positioning guides for the appliqué pieces (see **Photo 1**).

[3] Then fold the square appliqué foundation diagonally in both directions and lightly finger-press to make additional positioning guidelines (see **Photo 2**).

[4] Draw corresponding vertical, horizontal, and diagonal positioning guidelines on your full-size appliqué pattern if they are not already marked (see **Photo 3**).

[5] Prepare the appliqué pieces using the desired method. (See Preparing Appliqué Pieces beginning on *page 12*.) Referring to your appliqué pattern, pin and stitch the appliqué pieces to the foundation using your desired method; work from the bottom layer up.

[6] After the appliqué is complete, trim the appliqué foundation to the desired finished size plus seam allowances (see **Photo 4**).

1

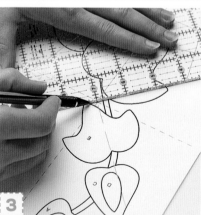

2

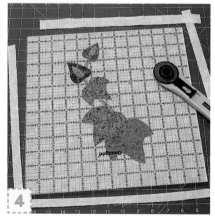

3

4

marked-foundation method

Cut the appliqué foundation fabric larger than the desired finished size to allow for any take-up in the fabric that might occur during the appliqué process. For example, for a 12" finished square, cut a 14"-square appliqué foundation. When the appliqué is complete, you'll trim the foundation square to 12½" square. (The extra ¼" on each side will be used for seam allowances when assembling the quilt top.)

Using a faint pencil line and your full-size appliqué pattern, trace the design onto the appliqué foundation fabric (see Photo 5). To avoid having markings show after the appliqué is complete, lightly mark just inside the design lines and just at critical points (for example, where two lines intersect or at the tips of leaves).

Prepare the appliqué pieces using the desired method. (See Preparing Appliqué Pieces beginning on *page 12*.) Referring to your appliqué pattern, pin and stitch the appliqué pieces to the foundation using your desired method; work from the bottom layer up.

After the appliqué is complete, trim the appliqué foundation to the desired size plus seam allowances.

light-box method

[1] Cut the appliqué foundation fabric larger than the desired finished size to allow for any take-up in the fabric that might occur during the appliqué process. For example, for a 12" finished square, cut a 14"-square appliqué foundation. When the appliqué is complete, you'll trim the foundation square to 12½" square. (The extra ¼" on each side will be used for seam allowances when assembling the quilt top.)

[2] Place your full-size appliqué pattern on a light box and secure it with tape (see Photo 6). Center the appliqué foundation fabric atop the appliqué pattern.

[3] Prepare the appliqué pieces using the desired method. (See Preparing Appliqué Pieces beginning on *page 12*.) Return to the light box and pin the bottom layer of appliqué pieces in place on the appliqué foundation (see Photo 7). Stitch the appliqué pieces to the foundation using your desired method.

[4] After stitching the bottom layer of appliqué pieces, return the appliqué foundation to the light box. Match the next layer of appliqué pieces with the pattern, pin, and stitch (see Photo 8). Continue in this manner until all appliqué pieces are stitched to the foundation.

[5] Trim the appliqué foundation to the desired size plus seam allowances.

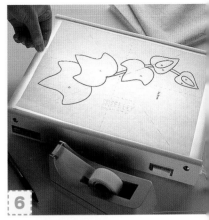

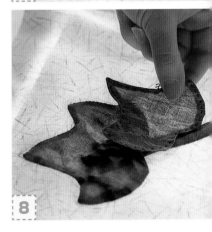

overlay method

[1] Cut the appliqué foundation fabric larger than the desired finished size to allow for any take-up in the fabric that might occur during the appliqué process. For example, for a 12" finished square, cut a 14"-square appliqué foundation. When the appliqué is complete, you'll trim the foundation square to 12½" square. (The extra ¼" on each side will be used for seam allowances when assembling the quilt top.)

[2] Position clear upholstery vinyl (or other clear flexible plastic) over your full-size appliqué pattern and precisely trace the design with a permanent marker (see **Photo 1**).

[3] Center the vinyl overlay on the appliqué foundation fabric. Pin the top of the overlay to the foundation (see **Photo 2**).

[4] Prepare the appliqué pieces using the desired method. (See Preparing Appliqué Pieces beginning on *page 12*.) Once the appliqué pieces have been prepared, slide the bottommost appliqué piece right side up between the appliqué foundation and the overlay (see **Photo 3**). When the piece is in place beneath its corresponding position on the vinyl overlay, remove the overlay and pin the appliqué piece to the foundation. Stitch the appliqué to the foundation using your desired method.

[5] Pin the vinyl overlay on the foundation and position the next appliqué piece in the stitching sequence (see **Photo 4**). Pin and stitch it to the foundation as before. Continue adding appliqué pieces in this manner until all appliqués have been stitched in place.

[6] Trim the appliqué foundation to the desired size plus seam allowances.

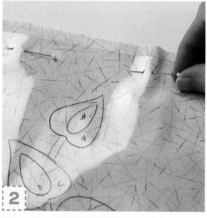

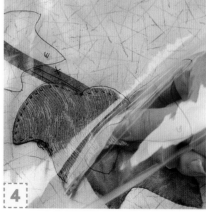

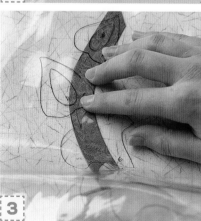

holding appliqué pieces in position

Once the appliqués and foundations have been prepared for stitching, the appliqué pieces can be held in place with pins, basting threads, spray adhesive, fabric glue stick, or fusible web. The number of appliqué layers you are working with may influence your choice.

PINS
Use as many straight pins as needed to hold each appliqué piece in place on the appliqué foundation for both machine and hand appliqué. Pins are generally used to hold no more than two layers at a time and are pushed through from the top. Some hand appliquérs like to place pins on the back side of the work to prevent catching thread in pins as they work. Remove the pins as you stitch.

BASTING
Sewing long stitches about ¼" from the turned-under edges is another way to secure prepared appliqué pieces to a foundation for both machine and hand appliqué. Begin and end the basting stitches on the right side of the appliqué for easier removal. You may wish to remove basting stitches when the entire appliqué work is complete or, if the basting threads impede stitching progress, remove them as you go. This is the preferred method of quilters who wish to hold multiple appliqué layers in position at once before permanently stitching them in place.

FABRIC BASTING SPRAY
When lightly sprayed on the wrong side of appliqué pieces, this adhesive usually allows you to position and reposition appliqués while you work. It can hold appliqués in place for both machine and hand appliqué. Work in a well-ventilated area and cover your work surface with paper. Be careful to spray lightly, as overspraying can cause a gummy buildup that makes stitching difficult.

FABRIC GLUE OR GLUE STICK
Apply these adhesives lightly to the wrong side of the prepared appliqué pieces along the outer edges or in the center. Press the appliqué piece to the appliqué foundation fabric. Be sure to apply the glue sparingly to avoid a buildup that would be difficult to stitch through. This method can be used for both machine and hand appliqué.

FUSIBLE WEB
This adhesive is most often used to hold pieces in position for machine appliqué. If you have an appliqué project with multiple layers of pieces that are prepared with fusible web, you may wish to hold them in position before adhering them to the foundation. To do so, place your full-size appliqué pattern beneath a clear, nonstick pressing sheet. Layer the prepared appliqué pieces in position right side up on the pressing sheet. Press lightly, just enough to fuse the pieces together, following the manufacturer's instructions. Do not slide the iron, but pick it up and move it from one area to the next. Let the pieces cool, then remove the fused appliqués from the pressing sheet and fuse them to the appliqué foundation.

hand appliqué

There are many ways to hand-stitch pieces in place on an appliqué foundation. If you're new to hand appliqué, experiment with each to determine which method is most comfortable for you.

For most hand appliqué, use a sharp, between, straw, or milliner's needle and the finest thread you can find that matches the appliqué pieces. The higher the number, the finer the thread, so look for silk or fine cotton machine-embroidery threads; they will make your appliqué stitches nearly invisible.

traditional appliqué stitch

This technique uses appliqué pieces that have had the seam allowances turned under. (For more information, see Preparing Appliqué Pieces beginning on *page 12*.)

For best results, use a sharp, between, straw, or milliner's needle.

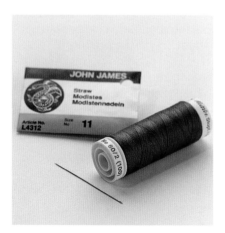

[1] Prepare the appliqué pieces by turning the seam allowances under. Pin, baste, or glue an appliqué piece in place on the appliqué foundation.

[2] Working with a length of thread no longer than 18", insert the needle into the wrong side of the appliqué foundation directly beneath the edge of the appliqué piece (see **Photo 1**). Bring the needle up through the rolled edge of the appliqué piece.

[3] Hold the needle parallel to the edge of the appliqué with the point of the needle next to the spot where the thread just exited (see **Photo 2**).

[4] Slide the point of the needle under the appliqué edge, into the appliqué foundation, and forward about $1/8$" to $3/16$", bringing the needle point out through the rolled edge of the appliqué (see **Photo 3**).

[5] Give the thread a gentle tug to bury the stitch in the fabric and allow the appliqué shape to rise up off the foundation (see **Photo 4**). Continue stitching in the same manner around the shape along the rolled edge.

[6] On the wrong side of the appliqué foundation, the stitches will be slightly angled (see **Photo 5**).

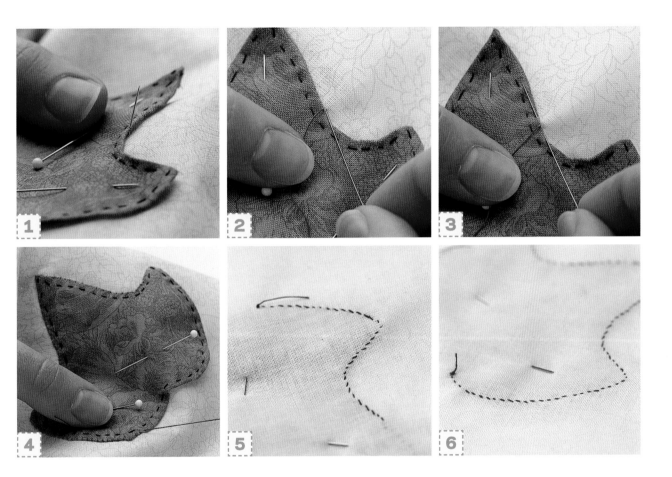

[7] End the thread by knotting it on the wrong side of the foundation, beneath the appliqué piece (see **Photo 6**).

[8] Once all pieces have been appliquéd, press the foundation from the wrong side and trim it to the desired size, including the seam allowances.

needle-turn appliqué

This technique involves turning under the appliqué seam allowance as you stitch. For best results, use a straw or milliner's needle. The extra length of these needles aids in tucking fabric under before taking stitches.

[1] Prepare the appliqué pieces following the Freezer-Paper Right-Side Method on *page 20*, or by completing steps 1 and 2 of the Basting Method on *page 12*. Pin, baste, or glue an appliqué piece in place on the appliqué foundation.

[2] Working with a length of thread no longer than 18", insert the needle into the wrong side of the appliqué foundation directly beneath the edge of the appliqué piece. Bring your needle up between the appliqué and the foundation. Use the point of the needle to sweep the seam allowance under about 1" or so ahead of your stitching and secure the fabric with your thumb. The edge of the freezer-paper template or the drawn line serves as your guide for how much to turn under (see **Photo 1**).

[3] Hold the needle parallel to the edge of the appliqué with the needle's point at the spot where the thread just exited.

Slide the point of the needle under a thread or two along the appliqué's rolled edge. Give the thread a gentle tug to bury the stitch in the fabric and allow the appliqué shape to rise up off the foundation (see **Photo 2**).

[4] Then place the tip of the needle into the appliqué foundation and rock it forward, bringing the tip up into the rolled appliqué edge about ⅛" to ³⁄₁₆" away from the previous stitch. Pull the needle through and gently tug the thread to bury the stitch as before.

[5] Continue in the same manner around the entire appliqué, taking tinier stitches around inside corners and curves where the seam allowances are more scant. Use the needle point to manipulate the seam allowance to lie flat in outside curves.

[6] End the thread by knotting it on the wrong side of the foundation, beneath the appliqué piece.

[7] Once all pieces have been appliquéd, press the foundation from the wrong side and trim it to the desired size, including the seam allowances.

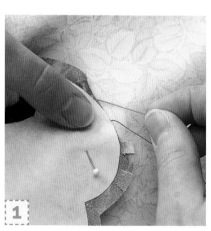

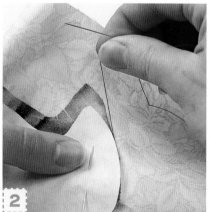

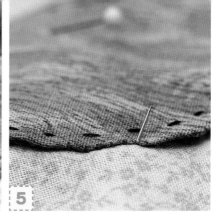

tack stitch

This technique uses appliqué pieces that have had the seam allowances turned. (For more information, see Preparing Appliqué Pieces beginning on *page 12*.) For best results, use a sharp, between, straw, or milliner's needle.

[1] Prepare the appliqué pieces by turning the seam allowances under. Pin, baste, or glue an appliqué piece in place on the appliqué foundation.

[2] Working with a length of thread no longer than 18", insert the needle into the wrong side of the appliqué foundation directly beneath the edge of the appliqué piece.

Bring the needle up through the rolled edge of the appliqué piece (see **Photo 3**).

[3] Insert the needle down into the foundation right next to the appliqué edge where it came up (see **Photo 4**).

[4] Bring the needle back up through the edge of the appliqué piece about $\frac{1}{16}$" from the first stitch. Continue in the same manner to stitch the appliqué piece to the foundation (see **Photo 5**).

[5] Once all pieces have been appliquéd, press the foundation from the wrong side and trim it to the desired size, including the seam allowances.

tips

- Work in a clockwise or counterclockwise direction, whichever is more comfortable for you.
- At inside points, make your stitches close together to prevent thread from raveling where you have clipped into the seam allowance. Secure an inside point with a single stitch.
- At an outside point, stitch right up to the point, then rotate the appliqué foundation and continue stitching down the next side.
- If the foundation fabric shows through the appliqué fabric, cut away the foundation beneath the appliqué after the stitching is complete. Carefully trim the underlying fabric to within $\frac{1}{4}$" of the stitching (see **Photo 6**). Be careful not to cut into the appliqué fabric.

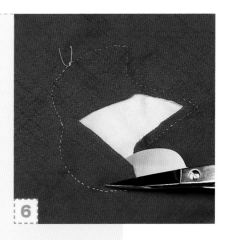

running stitch

This method results in a more primitive or folk art look. It uses appliqué pieces that have had the seam allowances turned under. (For more information, see Preparing Appliqué Pieces beginning on *page 12*.) For best results, use a sharp, between, straw, or milliner's needle.

[1] Prepare the appliqué pieces by turning the seam allowances under. Pin, baste, or glue an appliqué piece in place on the appliqué foundation.

[2] Working with a length of thread no longer than 18", insert the needle into the wrong side of the appliqué foundation directly beneath the edge of the appliqué piece. Bring the needle up through the appliqué piece about 1/16" from the rolled edge.

[3] Weave the needle in and out through both the edge of the appliqué piece and the foundation, staying about 1/16" from the outside edge of the appliqué (see **Photo 1**). Rock the needle in and out, taking small, evenly spaced stitches. Continue in this manner to secure the appliqué piece to the background.

[4] Working with perle cotton and a larger needle, you can produce a larger running stitch (see **Photo 2**), sometimes called a utility stitch or big stitch. The standard running stitch done in matching thread is shown in **Photo 2**, left.

[5] Once all pieces have been appliquéd, press the foundation from the wrong side and trim it to the desired size, including the seam allowances.

reverse appliqué

With this method, the foundation fabric is sewn on top of the appliqué fabric. The foundation is then cut away to reveal the appliqué fabric underneath. For best results, use a straw or milliner's needle.

[1] Make a template for each appliqué piece. (See Making Appliqué Templates on *page 10*.) Make an overlay for the complete appliqué pattern. (See Overlay Method on *page 24*.) **Note:** If you're making templates and overlays for letters and/or numbers, keep them on a straight baseline and mark the center point of each word or series of numbers.

[2] Mark the center of the foundation fabric. Position the overlay on the foundation fabric, aligning the marked centers. Pin the overlay in place. Slide a template under the overlay into position (see **Photo 3**).

[3] Flip back the overlay and, using an erasable marking tool, carefully trace around the template on the foundation fabric (see **Photo 4**).

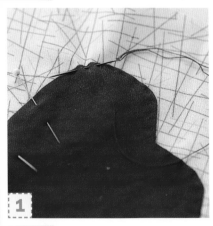

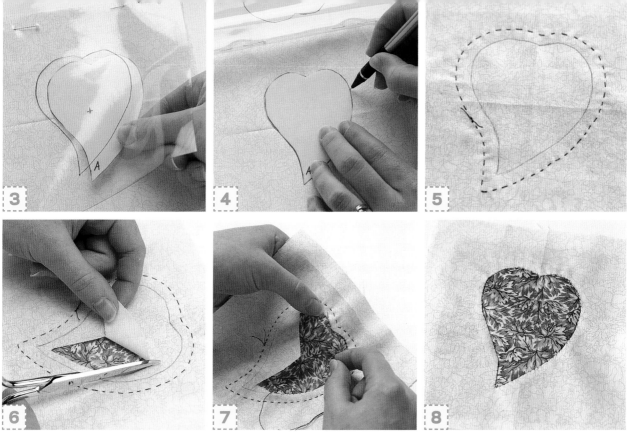

[4] Place the appliqué fabric right side up, directly beneath the traced motif on the foundation fabric. Baste around the outer edges of the motif, 5/16" away from the traced lines (see **Photo 5**).

[5] Starting in the middle of the motif, cut away a small portion of the foundation fabric, cutting 3/16" inside the traced line to create an edge for turning under (see **Photo 6**).

[6] Turn the raw edge under and slip-stitch the folded edge to the appliqué fabric beneath (see **Photo 7**). Clip curves as necessary to make the edge lie flat.

[7] Continue cutting away the foundation fabric a little at a time, turning under the raw edge and stitching the folded edge to the fabric below until you have revealed the entire motif (see **Photo 8**).

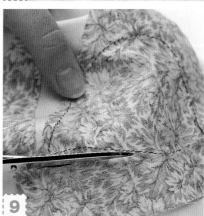

[8] Once you've completed the appliqué, turn it over and trim the appliqué fabric to within 1/4" of the seam allowance (see **Photo 9**).

[9] Press the foundation from the wrong side and trim to the desired size, including the seam allowances.

machine appliqué

There are numerous methods to machine appliqué pieces in place. The technique you choose should be based on the finished look you're after. For a mock-hand appliqué look, choose thread colors that match your appliqué shapes and a very narrow zigzag or blind-hem stitch. For bold stitching that outlines your appliqué shapes, you may prefer the look of dense satin stitching in a contrasting thread color. Or perhaps a decorative stitch, such as the blanket stitch, can add the folk-art look you want.

Regardless of the machine technique you choose, pay special attention to the tips given here for using stabilizers, rounding corners, turning at inside and outside points, and more. It's the attention to these details that will help you achieve flawless machine appliqué results.

beginning and ending stitching

[1] To begin stitching, bring the bobbin and needle threads to the top; this helps prevent thread tangles and snarls on the wrong side of your work. To begin this way, put the presser foot down and take one stitch. Stop and pull the bobbin thread to the top (see **Photo 1**).

[2] Set your machine for your desired stitch. Holding the bobbin and needle threads to one side, take a few stitches on a curve or straight edge; do not start at an inner or outer point (see **Photo 2**). (If your machine has a variable stitch length, you may wish to set your stitch length at 0 and take a few stitches, one on top of the next, to lock threads in

sewing machine setup for machine appliqué

- Make certain your machine is clean and in good working order.
- Install a new size 60/8, 70/10, 75/11, or 80/12 sharp embroidery needle in your machine.
- Wind a bobbin with cotton 60-weight embroidery thread or bobbin-fill thread.
- Thread the needle with matching- or complementary-color cotton 60-weight embroidery thread.
- Set your machine for a zigzag stitch with a width between 1 and 1.5 mm or about ⅛" wide. Set the stitch length just above (not at) the satin-stitch setting, or between .5 and 1 mm.
- If possible, set your machine in the "needle down" position, and set the motor at half speed.

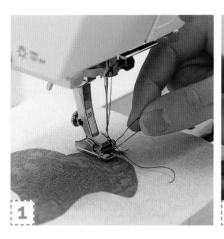

1

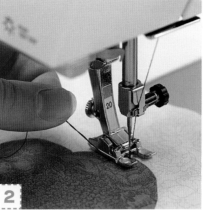

2

3

4

place at the start.) Reset your machine to the desired stitch setting; stitch about 1" and trim off the thread tails (see **Photo 3**). Or, when the appliqué work is completed, use a needle to draw the thread tails to the wrong side of the work and bury them in the stitching.

[3] To end, stitch one or two threads past the point where the stitching began and take one or two backstitches to secure the thread (see **Photo 4**). (If your machine has a variable stitch length, you may wish to set your stitch length at 0 and take a few stitches, one on top of the next, to lock the threads in place.)

tip

For machine appliqué, use a 60/8, 70/10, 75/11, or 80/12 sharp needle. For best results, use a smaller number needle for lighter weight, finer fabrics, and monofilament threads; use a larger number needle for medium-weight fabrics and cotton threads. Sewing on flannel or working with decorative threads requires larger or specialty needles.

mock hand appliqué

This method results in nearly invisible stitching that mimics the look of hand appliqué. To begin, set your machine for a variable overlock stitch or a blind hem stitch. If your sewing machine doesn't have this stitch, modify a standard zigzag stitch: Make it narrow and short, about 11 stitches per inch. Use a 50- or 60-weight, two-ply, cotton, machine-embroidery thread in colors that match the appliqué pieces, not the appliqué foundation. **Note:** Contrasting thread was used in the photos that follow for illustration purposes only.

[1] Prepare the appliqué pieces following the Spray-Starch Method on *page 18*.

[2] Position an appliqué piece so that the needle goes into the appliqué foundation right next to it. You may wish to use basting glue to hold appliqué pieces in place on the foundation. The needle should be so near the fold of the appliqué piece that it touches the fold but does not stitch through it (see **Photo 1**).

When the needle jumps to the left, the stitch should be totally on the appliqué piece (see **Photo 2**).

When the needle jumps to the right to complete a zigzag stitch, the needle should again be against the edge of the appliqué piece but go through the foundation only.

Sew right along the edge of the appliqué shape so one swing of the stitch goes into the foundation alongside the appliqué, and the other swing just catches the edge of the appliqué shape.

[3] When you come to inside and outside points, make sure to secure them with with several stitches. Make certain the needle always touches the fold of the appliqué so no edges are missed (see **Diagram 1**, *opposite*). When stitching small pieces, a stiletto or sharp seam ripper can be helpful to smooth out edges of appliqué pieces as you stitch.

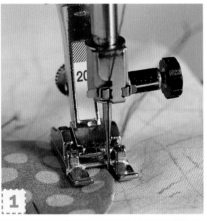

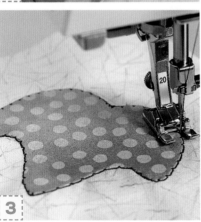

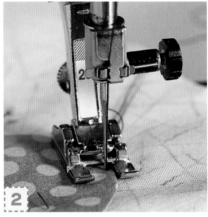

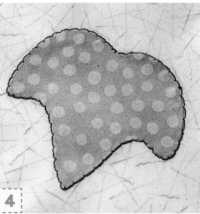

sewing machine setup for using monofilament thread

- Make certain your machine is clean and in good working order.
- Install a new size 60/8, 70/10, or 75/11 embroidery needle in your machine.
- Wind a bobbin with cotton 60-weight embroidery thread.
- Thread the needle with lightweight, invisible, nylon (monofilament) thread. Use clear thread for light-color fabrics; use smoke-color invisible thread for medium- and dark-color fabrics.
- Set your machine for a blind hem stitch with the stitch width and length each set at 1 mm. This stitch takes 2 to 5 straight stitches, then a zigzag, then 2 to 5 more straight stitches before zigzagging again.

Stitch a test sample using the same threads and fabrics as in your project. The distance between each zigzag should be ⅛" maximum, and the width of the zigzag should be the width of two threads.

When you are finished, you should be able to see the needle holes but no thread. If you gently pull on the edge of the appliqué, the stitching should be strong and without gaps.

Check the stitch tension on the test sample. There should be no bobbin thread showing on the top and no loops of nylon thread on the bottom. If the bobbin thread is showing on the top, loosen the top tension gradually until the bobbin thread no longer shows. Turn the sample over. If there are loops of nylon thread on the bottom, you've loosened the top tension too much.

[4] Continue stitching around the appliqué. When you reach the location where the stitching began, stitch over the beginning stitches to secure the threads. To lock your stitches, backstitch only two or three stitches (see **Photo 3**, *opposite*).

[5] When the stitching is complete, check all the edges of the appliqué to make sure no areas were left unstitched on the right side of the fabric (see **Photo 4**, *opposite*).

DIAGRAM 1

zigzag or satin stitch appliqué

Variable-width satin or zigzag stitch makes a smooth, professional-looking finish on appliqué edges. Choose a thread color that complements or matches your appliqué fabric. Select a stitch width that corresponds to the size of the piece being appliquéd. Larger pieces can accommodate a wider, denser appliqué stitch than smaller appliqué shapes can.

With a machine satin stitch, it is not necessary to turn under the appliqué piece's edges because the entire outer edge is held in place by the zigzag or satin stitch. The outer edge of the stitch just grazes the appliqué foundation. Depending upon the stability of your fabric, the appliqué design, and your personal preference, you can use fusible web, pins, or fabric glue to hold the appliqué pieces in place for machine stitching. Use a stabilizer behind the appliqué foundation (see About Stabilizers, *below*).

[1] Position the presser foot so that the left swing of the needle is on the appliqué and the right swing of the needle is just on the outer edge of the appliqué, grazing the appliqué foundation (see **Photo 1**).

[2] Begin stitching on a curve or straight edge, not at an inner or outer point (see **Photo 2**).

ABOUT STABILIZERS
Stabilizers are used beneath appliqué foundations to add support and eliminate puckers and pulling on the fabric as you machine-appliqué. Some stabilizers are temporary and are removed once stitching is complete (as in the photo, *right*, where the stabilizer is removed by holding it firmly on one side of the stitching and gently pulling it away from the other side). Others are permanent and remain in the quilt or are only partially cut away after stitching. Many brands are available. Two of the most common types are tear-away and water-soluble stabilizers. Freezer paper also may be used as a stabilizer. Experiment with a variety of types to determine which works best for you.

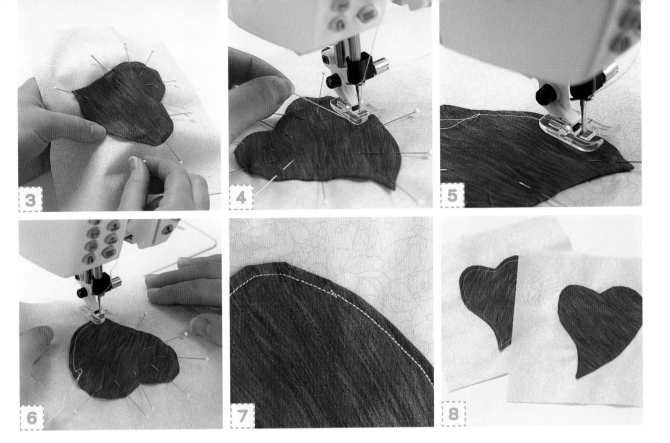

straight-stitch appliqué

[1] Prepare the appliqué pieces following the desired method. (For more information, see Preparing Appliqué Pieces beginning on *page 12*.) Pin, baste, or glue the appliqués in place (see **Photo 3**).

[2] Set the stitch length at 0. Beginning on a straight edge or a curve, take two or three stitches about ⅛" from the outer edge of the appliqué to anchor the thread. Hold the thread tails out of the way to prevent thread snarls on the underside (see **Photo 4**). Note: Remove pins before the needle reaches them.

[3] Adjust the stitch length to the desired number of stitches per inch (12 to 15) and continue sewing around the appliqué edge, staying ⅛" from the outer edge (see **Photo 5**).

[4] To stitch inner and outer curves, stop with the needle down, lift the presser foot, pivot the appliqué foundation, lower the presser foot, and continue sewing (see **Photo 6**).

[5] To end your stitching, gradually reduce the stitch length to 0 as you meet the point where the stitching began. Make the last two or three stitches next to the stitches where you started. Do not backstitch or overlap stitches (see **Photo 7**). **Note:** Contrasting thread was used in the photographs for illustration purposes only. In **Photo 8**, the sample shown on the *right* uses monofilament thread, so the stitching line does not appear as visible on the right side of the appliqué.

decorative stitch appliqué

This technique is often done on a sewing machine using the blanket or buttonhole stitch. Other decorative stitches also may be used, such as the featherstitch.

[1] Prepare the appliqué pieces following the desired method. (For more information, see Preparing Appliqué Pieces beginning on *page 12*.) Pin, baste, or glue the appliqués in place.

[2] Use a tear-away stabilizer beneath the appliqué foundation. (See About Stabilizers on *page 36*.)

[3] Beginning on a straight edge or a curve, take a few stitches; hold the thread tails out of the way to prevent thread snarls on the wrong side of your project. The right swing of the needle should graze the appliqué foundation. The left swing of the needle should be completely on the appliqué piece.

[4] For inside curves, stop with the needle down in the fabric on the left needle swing, lift the presser foot, pivot the appliqué foundation, lower the presser foot, and continue sewing (see **Photo 1**).

[5] For outside curves, stop with the needle down in the fabric on the right needle swing, lift the presser foot, pivot the appliqué foundation, and continue sewing (see **Photo 2**).

[6] Adjust the stitch length as necessary at corners and where the stitching meets at the end (see **Photo 3**).

pivoting at corners, curves, and points

The position of your needle is critical when pivoting fabric to round a curve or turn a point or corner. Use the following illustrations to guide you in knowing when to pivot. In each case, you will need to place your needle down in the fabric before pivoting. In each illustration the arrows indicate stitching direction, and the dots mark where the needle should be down for pivoting.

TURNING CORNERS—METHOD 1
With this method the stitches cross over one another in the corners.

[1] Stop with the needle down in the fabric on the right-hand swing of the needle (see **Diagram 1**).

[2] Raise the presser foot and pivot the fabric. Lower the presser foot and begin stitching to the next edge (see **Diagram 2**).

TURNING CORNERS—METHOD 2
With this method the stitching lines abut, but they do not cross over one another.

[1] Stop with the needle down in the fabric on the left-hand swing of the needle (see **Diagram 3**).

[2] Raise the presser foot and pivot the fabric. Lower the presser foot and turn the handwheel until the right-hand swing of the needle is just about to go into the foundation fabric. Lift the presser foot and reposition the foundation fabric so the tip of the needle is above the point where the needle thread is coming out of the

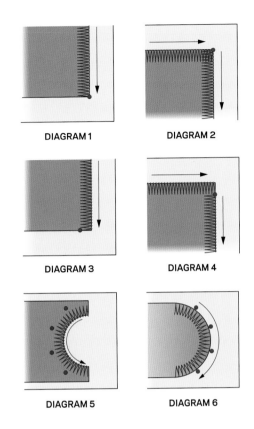

DIAGRAM 1   DIAGRAM 2

DIAGRAM 3   DIAGRAM 4

DIAGRAM 5   DIAGRAM 6

appliqué. Lower the presser foot and begin stitching to the next edge (see **Diagram 4**).

PIVOTING INSIDE CURVES
Stop at the first pivot point with the needle down in the fabric on the left-hand swing of the needle. Raise the presser foot, pivot the fabric slightly, and begin stitching to the next pivot point. Repeat as needed to round the entire inner curve (see **Diagram 5**).

PIVOTING OUTSIDE CURVES
Stop at the first pivot point with the needle down in the fabric on the right-hand swing of the needle. Raise the presser foot, pivot the fabric slightly, and begin stitching to the next pivot point. Repeat as needed to round the entire outer curve (see **Diagram 6**).

PIVOTING INSIDE POINTS

[1] With a marking tool, mark a line extending from the upcoming edge of the appliqué into the center. On the line, measure from the point a distance equal to your stitch width; mark the location with a dot (see **Diagram 1**).

[2] Stitch to the bottom of the inside point, stopping with the needle down in the fabric on the left-hand swing of the needle. The needle should be at the dot on your drawn marked line (see **Diagram 2**).

[3] Raise the presser foot and pivot the fabric. Lower the presser foot and turn the handwheel until the right-hand swing of the needle is just about to go into the foundation fabric. Lift the presser foot and reposition the foundation fabric so the tip of the needle is above the point where the needle thread is coming out of the appliqué. Lower the presser foot and begin stitching to the next edge (see **Diagram 3**).

PIVOTING OUTSIDE POINTS

Shapes with outside points are among the more difficult to appliqué. This method requires you to taper your stitch width at the point. If your project requires you to appliqué around this shape, practice first on scraps to perfect your technique.

[1] Stitch along the first edge of the appliqué, keeping the stitch width consistent until the left-hand swing of the needle begins to touch the opposite outside edge of the point. Stop with the needle down in the fabric on the left-hand swing of the needle (see **Diagram 4**).

[2] Gradually reduce your stitch width and continue sewing toward the point. Keep the right- and left-hand swings of the needle just grazing the outer edges and taper your stitch width until it's 0 at the point. Stop with the needle down in the fabric (see **Diagram 5**).

[3] Raise the presser foot and pivot the fabric. Lower the presser foot and begin stitching away from the point, increasing the stitch width at the same rate that you decreased it until you have returned to the original stitch width. Pivot the fabric slightly as needed to keep the right-hand swing of the needle grazing the foundation at the right-hand edge of the appliqué piece (see **Diagram 6**).

DIAGRAM 1

DIAGRAM 2

DIAGRAM 3

DIAGRAM 4

DIAGRAM 5

DIAGRAM 6

machine appliqué troubleshooting tips

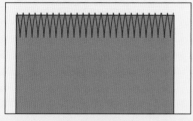

This machine-appliqué stitching is correctly placed. The outside edge of the stitch is just grazing the appliqué foundation.

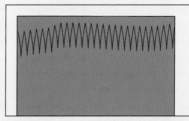

This stitching is too far inside the edge of the appliqué piece, so fabric threads from the appliqué will fray and poke out around the edges.

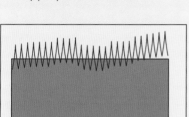

Here the stitches are too far outside the edge of the appliqué piece, so it may pull loose from the foundation.

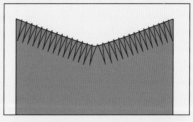

Gaps will occur in the stitching if your needle is down in the fabric on the wrong side of the needle swing when you pivot.

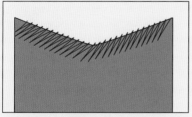

Your stitches will slant if you try to pull or push the fabric through curves, rather than lifting the presser foot and pivoting the fabric.

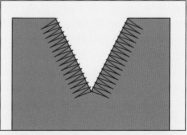

Pivoting too soon on an inside point will leave an incomplete line of stitches at the point.

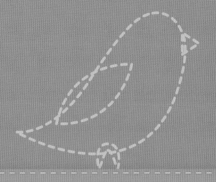
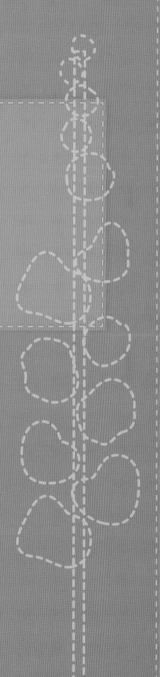
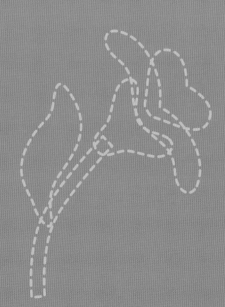

easy

Start appliquéing with this collection of beginner-friendly projects.

petalpushers

Give the appliqués on this table runner a raised effect using batting and freezer paper. Complete the look by whipping up a set of coordinating napkins.

DESIGNER **RHODA NELSON**   PHOTOGRAPHER **ADAM ALBRIGHT**

materials

Quantities are for one table runner and four napkins.

- ¼ yard multicolor dot (appliqués)
- ½ yard green polka dot (appliqués, binding)
- 1⅞ yards multicolor stripe (appliqués, backing)
- ⅛ yard purple polka dot (appliqués)
- 1⅞ yards solid white (appliqué foundation, napkin lining)
- 1 yard each of white-and-lavender dot and white-and-green dot (napkins)
- 32×66" batting
- Freezer paper

Finished table runner: 16×60"
Finished napkins: 15" square

Quantities are for 44/45"-wide, 100% cotton fabrics. **Measurements** include ¼" seam allowances. Sew with right sides together unless otherwise stated.

cut fabrics

Cut pieces in the following order. Cut backing and appliqué foundation rectangles lengthwise (parallel to the selvages).

The Leaf Pattern is on *Pattern Sheet 1*. To make a template of the pattern, see Making and Using Templates beginning on *page 10*. When cutting fabric shapes from Leaf Pattern, be sure to add a ¼" seam allowance beyond the drawn line. When cutting batting shapes from Leaf Pattern, cut directly on the drawn line.

From multicolor dot, cut:
- 21 of Leaf Pattern

From green polka dot, cut:
- 4—2½×42" binding strips
- 9 of Leaf Pattern

From multicolor stripe, cut:
- 1—22×66" backing rectangle
- 6 of Leaf Pattern

From purple polka dot, cut:
- 6 of Leaf Pattern

From solid white, cut:
- 1—18×62" rectangle for appliqué foundation
- 4—15½" squares

From white-and-lavender dot, cut:
- 4—15½" squares

From white-and-green dot, cut:
- 4—15½" squares

From batting, cut:
- 1—22×66" rectangle
- 42 of Leaf Pattern

prepare appliqués

Designer Rhoda Nelson used a freezer-paper method for appliquéing. (For more information, see Freezer-Paper Wrong-Side Method 1, *page 14*.) To use this method, complete the following steps.

[1] Lay freezer paper, shiny side down, over Leaf Pattern. Use a pencil to trace pattern 42 times, leaving at least ½" between shapes. Cut out freezer-paper shapes on drawn lines.

[2] Center a batting piece and a freezer-paper template with shiny side up on the wrong side of multicolor dot leaf (**Diagram 1**).

DIAGRAM 1

DIAGRAM 2

DIAGRAM 3

[3] Using tip of a hot dry iron, press fabric seam allowance over edge of freezer paper, ensuring fabric is taut against template. For sharp outer points, first fold fabric straight over points of freezer-paper template (**Diagram 2**). Then press under remaining edges (**Diagram 3**). The seam allowance will adhere to the freezer paper. (Do not touch iron soleplate to freezer paper past turned fabric edge.)

[4] Repeat steps 2 and 3 to prepare remaining multicolor dot, green polka dot, multicolor stripe, and purple polka dot leaf appliqués.

appliqué table runner top

[1] Referring to photo, *right*, position leaf appliqués on solid white 18×62" appliqué foundation in a gentle curve; pin appliques in place.

[2] Using thread that matches appliqués and a small slip stitch, hand-appliqué around most of a leaf appliqué. Carefully peel off freezer-paper template and discard, then finish sewing around leaf. Stitch around each leaf in same manner to complete table runner top.

finish table runner

[1] Layer table runner top and batting and backing rectangles; baste. (For details, see Complete the Quilt, *page 159*.)

[2] Quilt as desired. To further enhance the raised effect, outline-quilt around each leaf appliqué. The featured quilt was machine-quilted with an allover swirl pattern on the remainder of the quilt top (**Quilting Diagram**).

[3] Trim quilted table runner to 16×60" including seam allowances. Bind with green polka dot binding strips. (For details, see Complete the Quilt.)

assemble napkins

[1] With right sides together, layer a white-and-lavender dot 15½" square and a white-and-green dot 15½" square. Place a solid white 15½" square atop layered squares; press. (The third layer of solid white prevents show-through on this reversible napkin and gives it more stability.)

[2] Sew together around all edges, leaving an 8" opening for turning in the middle of one edge (**Diagram 4**). Clip across each corner. Turn right side out and press. Hand-stitch opening closed.

[3] Topstitch ⅛" and 1" from all edges to complete napkin.

[4] Repeat steps 1–3 to make four napkins total.

QUILTING DIAGRAM

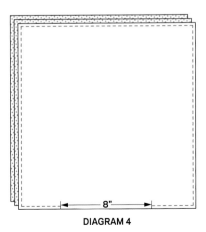

8"

DIAGRAM 4

fun house

Go collage crazy by showcasing an artful abode made from simple piecing, appliqués, and quirky embellishments in a coordinating decoupage frame.

DESIGNER **BARI J. ACKERMAN**   PHOTOGRAPHER **CAMERON SADEGHPOUR**

materials

- ▸ Scraps of assorted pastel multicolor stripe; aqua tone-on-tone; yellow, aqua, and cream prints; aqua polka dot; yellow florals; and aqua multicolor stripe (block, frame)
- ▸ Thread: pink
- ▸ Purchased 9½×11½" wood frame with 1"-wide edges and a 7½×9½" opening (available at framing and crafts supply stores)
- ▸ Stabilizer
- ▸ ⅜"-diameter button: tan
- ▸ Parchment or waxed paper
- ▸ Vintage brooch (optional)
- ▸ Appliqué glue (optional)
- ▸ Fabric glue
- ▸ Decoupage medium
- ▸ Foam brush

Finished project: 9½×11½"
Finished block: 8×10" (includes seam allowances)

Quantities are for 100% cotton fabrics. Measurements include ¼" seam allowances. Sew with right sides together unless otherwise stated.

cut fabrics

Cut pieces in the following order.

From pastel multicolor stripe, cut:
- ▸ 1—2⅞" square

From aqua tone-on-tone, cut:
- ▸ 1—2⅞" square

From yellow print, cut:
- ▸ 1—4½×5½" rectangle

From assorted aqua prints, cut:
- ▸ 1—8×3" rectangle
- ▸ 2—2¼×7½" rectangles

From cream print, cut:
- ▸ 6—1" squares

From aqua polka dot, cut:
- ▸ 1—1×9" strip
- ▸ 1—1×2" rectangle

From assorted yellow florals, cut:
▸ 2—1×9½" strips

From aqua multicolor stripe, cut:
▸ 1—1×9" strip

assemble house block

[1] Use a pencil to mark a diagonal line on wrong side of pastel multicolor stripe 2⅞" square. (To prevent fabric from stretching as you draw the line, place 220-grit sandpaper under the square.)

[2] Layer marked 2⅞" square atop aqua tone-on-tone 2⅞" square. Sew together with two seams, stitching ¼" on each side of the drawn line (**Diagram 1**).

[3] Cut pair apart on the drawn line to make two triangle units (**Diagram 1**). Open triangle units and press seams toward aqua tone-on-tone triangles to make two triangle-squares. Each triangle-square should be 2½" square including seam allowances.

[4] Referring to **Diagram 2**, join triangle-squares to make roof unit. Press seam in one direction. The roof unit should be 2½×4½" including seam allowances.

[5] Sew together roof unit and yellow print 4½×5½" rectangle to make house unit (**Block Assembly Diagram**). Press seam toward yellow print rectangle.

[6] Add aqua print 2¼×7½" rectangles to long edges of house unit. Press seams toward aqua print rectangles.

[7] Referring to **Block Assembly Diagram**, sew aqua print 8×3" rectangle to top edge of house unit. Press seam toward aqua print rectangle to make house block. The block should be 8×10" including seam allowances.

appliqué and embellish block

[1] Referring to **Appliqué Placement Diagram**, arrange six cream print 1" squares (windows) and one aqua polka dot 1×2" rectangle (door) on house block. If desired, hold each piece in place with a dot of appliqué glue.

[2] Using pink thread and a stabilizer under house block, machine-blanket-stitch around each appliqué shape. Remove stabilizer from back of block.

[3] Referring to photo on *page 49*, sew tan button to aqua polka dot door to complete appliquéd house block.

DIAGRAM 1

DIAGRAM 2

mount block

Remove backing board and glass (if included; set aside for another use) from frame. Run a narrow line of fabric glue along front edges of backing board. Smooth block to glue-edged backing board. Let dry on flat surface.

embellish frame and finish project

[1] Cover work surface with parchment paper or waxed paper. Using a foam brush, apply a thin coat of decoupage medium to surface edge of frame.

[2] Referring to photo on *page 49* for placement, while frame is still "wet," center aqua multicolor stripe 1×9" strip on one long surface edge of prepared frame. Using your finger or a brayer, smooth fabric strip to remove air bubbles or bumps. Repeat, adding aqua polka dot 1×9" strip to remaining long surface edge and yellow floral 1×9½" strips to top and bottom surface edges. Brush a coat of decoupage medium over fabric strips. Let dry overnight or until decoupage medium is clear and no longer sticky.

[3] If desired, repeat steps 1 and 2 using assorted fabric strips cut to fit return edges of frame.

[4] Insert mounted house block into frame to complete the project.

[5] If desired, add vintage brooch to house block.

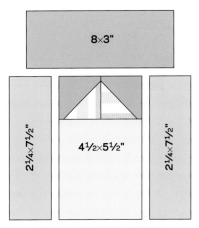

BLOCK ASSEMBLY DIAGRAM

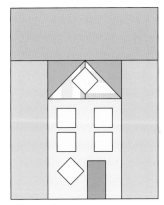

APPLIQUÉ PLACEMENT DIAGRAM

hollyhock
harvest

Appliqué a tall stem of flowers among large, machine-quilted patchwork pieces to make a stunning wall hanging.

DESIGNER **KRIS KERRIGAN**   DESIGNER **KAREN SELEY**
PHOTOGRAPHER **GREG SCHEIDEMANN**

materials

- ⅜ yard solid green (blocks, appliqués)
- ⅜ yard red print (blocks, appliqués)
- ½ yard cream print (appliqué foundation, sashing)
- ⅔ yard dark green print (blocks)
- 18×22" piece (fat quarter) green print (blocks)
- 18×22" piece (fat quarter) each light coral and dark coral prints (blocks)
- ⅔ yard light green print (blocks)
- ¾ yard brown print (border, binding)
- 2⅔ yards backing fabric
- 56×47" batting
- Lightweight fusible web
- 56—size 6 seed beads:cream or pale gold
- Embroidery floss: dark green, assorted light coral, cream

Finished quilt: 50×41"

Quantities are for 44/45"-wide, 100% cotton fabrics. **Measurements** include ¼" seam allowances. Sew with right sides together unless otherwise stated.

cut fabrics

To make the best use of your fabrics, cut pieces in the following order. Patterns are on *Pattern Sheet 1*.

To use fusible web for appliquéing, complete the following steps. (For more information, see Fusible-Web Method, *page 21*.)

[1] Lay fusible web, paper side up, over patterns. Use a pencil to trace each pattern the number of times indicated in cutting instructions, leaving ½" between tracings. Cut out each fusible-web shape roughly ¼" outside traced lines.

[2] Following the manufacturer's instructions, press fusible-web shapes onto backs of designated fabrics; let cool.

[3] Cut out fabric shapes on drawn lines and peel off paper backings.

From solid green, cut:
- 1—11½" square
- 1—¾×34" stem strip
- 2 each of patterns A, C, and G
- 1 of Pattern B

From red print, cut:
- 2—2½×17" strips
- 4—2½" squares
- 2 each of patterns D and F
- 3 of Pattern E

From cream print, cut:
- 1—7½×38½" rectangle
- 2—2½×17" strips
- 1—2½" square

From dark green print, cut:
- 1—22½×14½" rectangle
- 1—18½×7½" rectangle

From green print, cut:
- 1—18½×10½" rectangle

From light coral print, cut:
- 1—18½×7½" rectangle

From dark coral print, cut:
- 1—11½" square

From light green print, cut:
- 1—11½×22½" rectangle
- 1—18½×10½" rectangle

From brown print, cut:
- 5—2¼×42" binding strips
- 5—1¾×42" strips for border

From fusible web, cut:
- 1—¾×34" strip

appliqué hollyhock block

[1] Referring to **Quilt Assembly Diagram**, lay out pieces A–G and the solid green stem on cream print 7½×38½" rectangle. Fuse in place.

[2] Using thread that matches the appliqués and working from bottom to top, machine-blanket-stitch around appliqués to make the appliquéd block.

assemble sashing strips

[1] Referring to **Sashing Segment Assembly Diagram**, join two red print 2½×17" strips and two cream print 2½×17" strips to make a strip set. Press seams in one direction. Cut strip set into six 2½"-wide segments.

[2] Alternating colors, sew together two 2½"-wide segments and a red print 2½" square to make a short sashing strip; press seams in one direction. Repeat to make a second short sashing strip.

[3] Join two 2½"-wide segments, two red print 2½" squares, and a cream print 2½" square to make a long sashing strip. Press seams in one direction.

assemble quilt center

[1] Referring to **Quilt Assembly Diagram**, lay out rectangles, squares, and sashing strips in three vertical rows.

[2] Sew together pieces in left and right rows. Press seams in one direction. Add rows to appliquéd block to make quilt center. Press seams toward appliquéd block. The quilt center should be 47½×38½" including seam allowances.

assemble and add border

[1] Cut and piece brown print 1¾×42" strips to make:
- 2—1¾×50" border strips
- 2—1¾×38½" border strips

[2] Sew short border strips to short edges of quilt center. Add long border strips to remaining edges to complete quilt top. Press all seams toward border.

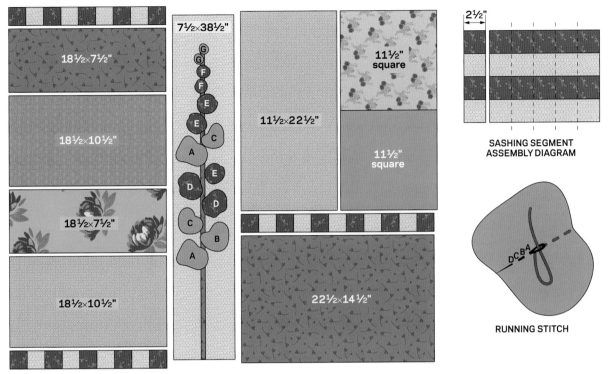

18½×7½"

18½×10½"

18½×7½"

18½×10½"

7½×38½"

G
G
F
F
E
E
C
A
E
D
D
C
B
A

11½×22½"

**11½"
square**

**11½"
square**

22½×14½"

QUILT ASSEMBLY DIAGRAM

2½"

SASHING SEGMENT
ASSEMBLY DIAGRAM

DCBA

RUNNING STITCH

finish quilt

[1] Layer quilt top, batting, and backing. (For details, see Complete the Quilt, *page 159*.)

[2] Quilt as desired. The featured quilt has a variety of designs machine-quilted across the quilt top to add texture.

[3] Bind with brown print binding strips. (For details, see Complete the Quilt.)

embellish quilt

Use three strands of embroidery floss for all stitches. Referring to leaf and flower patterns as a guide, hand-quilt running stitches on leaves and flowers using dark green floss on the leaves and assorted coral floss on the flowers.

To make a running stitch, pull your needle up at A and insert it back into the fabric at B (see diagram *above*). Continue in the same manner, loading several stitches on your needle at a time.

To add beads, thread a needle with 18" of cream embroidery floss and knot one floss end. Bring the needle up from the back at the center of a large flower, burying the knot in the batting. Thread five cream beads onto the needle, then insert the needle tip back into the fabric close to the end bead. Repeat to make three rows of beads side by side at the center of each large flower.

Add two rows of three beads each at the center of each medium flower. Add two rows of two beads each at the center of each small flower.

paisley craze

Appliqué dots and paisley shapes give this easy table topper a dash of modern flair.

DESIGNERS **CORI DERKSON** AND **MYRA HARDER**   QUILT MAKER **RHODA NELSON**   PHOTOGRAPHER **GREG SCHEIDEMANN**

materials

- ▸ 1 yard mottled white (appliqué foundation)
- ▸ ¼ yard green print (inner border, appliqués)
- ▸ 1 yard mottled gold (middle and outer borders)
- ▸ ⅞ yard teal print (outer border, appliqués, binding)
- ▸ ¼ yard gold print (appliqués)
- ▸ Scraps of pink print and light teal print (appliqués)
- ▸ 3 yards backing fabric
- ▸ 50" square batting
- ▸ Lightweight fusible web
- ▸ Clear monofilament thread

Finished quilt: 44½" square

Quantities are for 44/45"-wide, 100% cotton fabrics. **Measurements** include a ¼" seam allowance. Sew with right sides together unless otherwise stated.

cut fabrics

To make the best use of your fabrics, cut pieces in the following order. Pattern pieces are on *Pattern Sheet 4*.

To use fusible web for appliquéing, complete the following steps. (For more information, see Fusible-Web Method, *page 21*.)

[1] Lay fusible web, paper side up, over patterns. Use a pencil to trace each pattern the number of times indicated in cutting instructions, leaving at least ½" between tracings. Cut out each fusible-web shape roughly ¼" outside traced lines.

[2] Following the manufacturer's instructions, press fusible-web shapes onto backs of designated fabrics; let cool.

[3] Cut out fabric shapes on drawn lines and peel off paper backings.

From mottled white, cut:
- ▸ 1—31" square for quilt center

From green print, cut:
- ▸ 2—1½×33" inner border strips
- ▸ 2—1½×31" inner border strips
- ▸ 13 of Pattern D

From mottled gold, cut:
- ▸ 2—4¼×40½" middle border strips
- ▸ 2—4¼×33" middle border strips
- ▸ 10—5¼" squares, cutting each diagonally twice in an X for 40 large triangles total

From teal print, cut:
- ▸ 5—2½×42" binding strips
- ▸ 9—5¼" squares, cutting each diagonally twice in an X for 36 large triangles total
- ▸ 4—2⅞" squares, cutting each in half diagonally for 8 small triangles total
- ▸ 4—2½" squares
- ▸ 9 of Pattern A

From gold print, cut:
- ▸ 9 of Pattern B

From pink print, cut:
- ▸ 15 of Pattern C
- ▸ 9 of Pattern D

From light teal print, cut:
- ▸ 12 of Pattern E

add inner and middle borders

[1] Sew short green print inner border strips to opposite edges of mottled white 31" square. Add long green print inner border strips to remaining edges. Press all seams toward border.

[2] Join short mottled gold middle border strips to opposite edges of quilt center. Add long mottled gold middle border strips to remaining edges. Press all seams toward middle border.

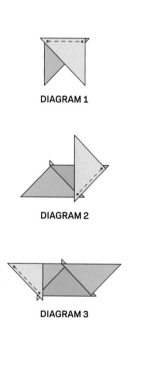

DIAGRAM 1

DIAGRAM 2

DIAGRAM 3

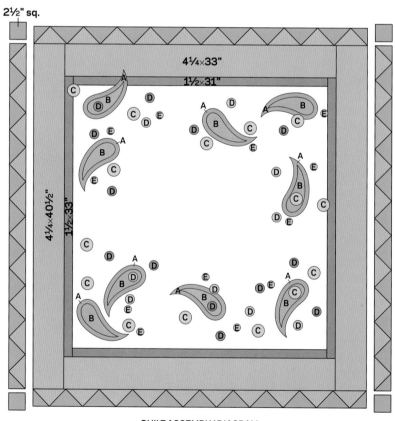

2½" sq.

4¼×33"

1½×31"

4¼×40½"

1½×33"

QUILT ASSEMBLY DIAGRAM

appliqué quilt center

Referring to **Quilt Assembly Diagram**, lay out appliqué pieces A–E on quilt center; fuse in place. Using clear monofilament thread, machine-zigzag-stitch around each appliqué.

assemble and add outer border

[1] Referring to **Quilt Assembly Diagram**, lay out two teal print small triangles, nine teal print large triangles, and 10 mottled gold large triangles in a row.

[2] Layer first two large triangles in the row with ends offset by ¼"; sew together to make a triangle pair (**Diagram 1**). Press seam toward teal triangle. Add next large triangle to triangle pair (**Diagram 2**). Press seam toward triangle just added. Add remaining large triangles in same manner. Add a small triangle to each end to complete the row (**Diagram 3**). Repeat to make four outer border strips total.

[3] Referring to **Quilt Assembly Diagram**, sew outer border strips to opposite edges of appliquéd quilt center. Press seams toward middle border.

[4] Sew a teal print 2½" square to each end of remaining outer border strips. Press seams toward teal squares. Join outer border strips to remaining edges of quilt center to complete quilt top. Press seams toward outer border.

finish quilt

[1] Layer quilt top, batting, and backing; baste. (For details, see Complete the Quilt, *page 159.*)

[2] Quilt as desired. The featured quilt was machine-quilted with an allover feather design. The paisley appliqués are outline-stitched to echo their shape; multicolored circles are stitched in a spiral motif.

[3] Bind with teal print binding strips. (For details, see Complete the Quilt.)

perk me up

Sweeten your morning coffee time with a wrap-around cozy in your choice of three tempting varieties.

DESIGNER **VERONICA KOH EISCHEID**   PHOTOGRAPHER **CAMERON SADEGHPOUR**

materials for drink cozy

- ▸ 5—2×3" rectangles assorted prints (appliqués)
- ▸ 6×12" rectangle solid tan (appliqué foundation)
- ▸ 6×12" rectangle orange print (lining)
- ▸ 6×12" rectangle cotton batting
- ▸ Lightweight fusible web
- ▸ Embroidery floss: brown
- ▸ Elastic ponytail keeper
- ▸ ⅞"-diameter button: brown
- ▸ Water-soluble pen
- ▸ Toothpick or wooden match

Finished cozy: 3½×10"

Quantities are for 100% cotton fabrics. **Measurements** include ½" seam allowances. Sew with right sides together unless otherwise stated.

prepare template and appliqués

Pattern pieces are on *Pattern Sheet 2*. To make a template of Pattern A, see Making Applique Templates on *page 10*.

To use fusible web for appliquéing letter patterns D,R, I, N, and K and patterns B through E, complete the following steps. (For more information on fusible appliqué, see Fusible-Web Method, *page 21*.)

[1] Lay fusible web, paper side up, over patterns. Use a pencil to trace each pattern the number of times indicated in cutting instructions, leaving ½" between tracings. Cut out fusible-web shapes roughly ¼" outside traced lines.

[2] Following the manufacturer's instructions, press fusible-web shapes onto wrong sides of designated fabrics; let cool. Cut out fabric shapes on drawn lines. Peel off paper backings.

cut fabrics for drink cozy

From assorted prints, cut:
- ▸ 1 each of patterns D, R, I, N, and K

From solid tan, cut:
- ▸ 1 of Pattern A

From orange print, cut:
- ▸ 1 of Pattern A

From batting, cut:
- ▸ 1 of Pattern A

appliqué drink cozy

[1] Referring to **Appliqué Placement Diagram**, arrange assorted print letters D, R, I, N, and K on solid tan A foundation. Fuse in place.

[2] Using five strands of brown embroidery floss, backstitch along outside and inside edges of fused letters to make appliquéd cozy top.

APPLIQUÉ PLACEMENT DIAGRAM

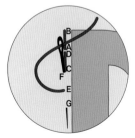

BACKSTITCH DIAGRAM

To backstitch, refer to **Backstitch Diagram** and pull needle up at A. Insert it back into fabric at B, and bring it up at C. Push needle down again at D, and bring it up at E. Continue in same manner.

assemble drink cozy

[1] Place A template on right side of appliquéd cozy top. Using water-soluble pen, transfer marked X to cozy top.

[2] Pinch ponytail keeper in half and pin to right side of cozy top, matching center with X and placing ⅞" of ponytail keeper loop extended toward cozy center (**Diagram 1**). Zigzag-stitch ponytail keeper center in place over marked X. (Depending on the elasticity of the ponytail keeper, you might need to make the length of the loop longer or shorter than ⅞". Baste ponytail keeper in place; slip button through loop to test elasticity.)

[3] With right sides together, layer appliquéd cozy top atop orange print A piece. Place layered pieces on top of A batting piece. Using ½" seam, sew around edges, leaving a 3" opening along bottom edge for turning (**Diagram 2**).

Trim seam allowance to ¼". On curved edges, clip notches in the seam allowance up to, but not through, stitching line. Turn cozy right side out through opening. Press flat and hand-stitch opening closed. Topstitch ⅛" from outer edge to make cozy.

[4] Snugly wrap cozy around desired coffee cup and pull ponytail keeper loop slightly taut. While pulling on loop, use water-soluble pen to mark a dot just inside end of loop on cozy's right side (**Diagram 3**). Remove cozy from cup.

[5] Align center of button with marked dot. Place a toothpick or wooden match on top of button. Sew button to right side of cozy, working stitches over toothpick or wooden match to make a button shank (**Diagram 4**). Remove toothpick or match. Pull button up tight against the extra sewn thread. Work needle through one of the buttonholes to back side of button. Wind thread around thread shank created below button. Secure and knot thread on lining side to complete the Drink Cozy.

materials for java banner cozy

- 4—2½×3" rectangles assorted prints (appliqués)
- 6×12" rectangle brown print (appliqué foundation)
- 6×12" rectangle aqua print (lining)
- 6×12" rectangle cotton batting
- Lightweight fusible web
- Lightweight, tearaway stabilizer
- Embroidery floss: brown
- Elastic ponytail keeper
- ⅞"-diameter button: orange
- Water-soluble pen
- Toothpick or wooden match

DIAGRAM 1

DIAGRAM 2

DIAGRAM 3

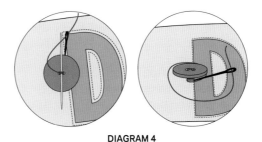

DIAGRAM 4

Finished cozy: 3¾×10"

Refer to Prepare Template and Appliqués on page 60 before cutting.

cut fabrics for java banner cozy

From assorted prints, cut:
‣ 4 of Pattern B
From brown print, cut:
‣ 1 of Pattern A
From aqua print, cut:
‣ 1 of Pattern A
From batting, cut:
‣ 1 of Pattern A

appliqué java banner cozy

[1] Full-Size Embroidery Patterns are on *Pattern Sheet 2*. Using a light box or window and a water-soluble pen, mark letters on assorted print B triangles.

[2] Referring to **Appliqué Placement Diagram**, arrange assorted print B triangles on brown print A foundation. Fuse in place.

[3] Using contrasting thread and a stabilizer under foundation, machine-straight-stitch around each appliqué piece. Remove stabilizer.

[4] Using water-soluble pen, draw banner string across top of each flag, from one edge of foundation to the other (**Appliqué Placement Diagram**). Following drawn line, machine-straight-stitch three closely spaced rows.

[5] Using four strands of brown embroidery floss, backstitch one marked letter on each appliquéd triangle to make appliquéd cozy top.

assemble java banner cozy

Referring to Assemble Drink Cozy, *page 62*, use appliquéd cozy top, aqua print A piece, A batting piece, ponytail keeper, and button to complete the Java Banner Cozy.

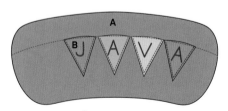

APPLIQUÉ PLACEMENT DIAGRAM

materials for trio of cups cozy

- 3—4" squares assorted prints (appliqués)
- 6×12" rectangle solid brown (appliqué foundation)
- 6×12" rectangle orange print (lining)
- 6×12" rectangle cotton batting
- Lightweight fusible web
- Lightweight, tearaway stabilizer
- Elastic ponytail keeper
- ⅞"-diameter button: aqua
- Water-soluble pen
- Toothpick or wooden match

Finished cozy: 3¾×10"

Refer to Prepare Template and Appliqués on page 60 before cutting.

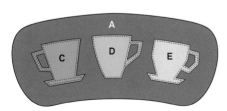

APPLIQUÉ PLACEMENT DIAGRAM

cut fabrics for trio of cups cozy

From assorted prints, cut:
- 1 each of patterns C, D, and E

From solid brown, cut:
- 1 of Pattern A

From orange print, cut:
- 1 of Pattern A

From batting, cut:
- 1 of Pattern A

appliqué trio of cups cozy

[1] Referring to **Appliqué Placement Diagram**, arrange assorted print C, D, and E cups on solid brown A foundation. Fuse in place.

[2] Using contrasting thread and a stabilizer under foundation, machine-straight-stitch around each appliqué piece to make appliquéd cozy top. Remove stabilizer.

assemble trio of cups cozy

Referring to Assemble Drink Cozy, *page 62*, use appliquéd cozy top, orange print A piece, A batting piece, ponytail keeper, and button to complete the Trio of Cups Cozy.

sew many
stitches

Try your hand at wool applique by making this pillow embellished with embroidery floss, beads, and buttons.

PHOTOGRAPHER **CAMERON SADEGHPOUR**

materials

- 1⅛ yards tan homespun (appliqué foundation, pillow back)
- 5½×12½" piece brown felted wool (basket appliqué)
- 3×26" piece green plaid felted wool (stem appliqués)
- Scraps of assorted felted wool in dark green, pink, purple, red, blue, yellow, and orange (appliqués)
- 130—size 8/0 seed beads: black
- Beading needle
- 3—½"-diameter buttons: brown
- Embroidery floss: brown, green, gold, purple, blue, red
- 12×20" pillow form
- Freezer paper

Finished Pillow: 12×20"

Quantities are for 44/45"-wide, 100% cotton and wool fabrics. **Measurements** include ¼" seam allowances. Sew with right sides together unless otherwise stated.

cut fabrics

Cut pieces in the following order. Pattern pieces are on *Pattern Sheet 1*.

Felted wool (available in many quilt shops) doesn't fray, so there is no need to turn under the cut edges of the pieces. To felt your own wool, machine-wash woven wool fabric in a hot-water wash, cool-rinse cycle with a small amount of detergent; machine-dry on high heat and steam-press.

To use freezer-paper templates for cutting appliqué pieces, complete the following steps.

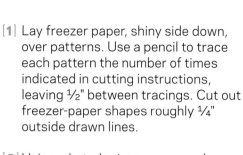

[1] Lay freezer paper, shiny side down, over patterns. Use a pencil to trace each pattern the number of times indicated in cutting instructions, leaving ½" between tracings. Cut out freezer-paper shapes roughly ¼" outside drawn lines.

[2] Using a hot, dry iron, press each freezer-paper shape, shiny side down, onto right side of designated fabric; let cool. Cut out fabric shapes on drawn lines. Peel off freezer paper.

From tan homespun, cut:
▸ 2—13×24" rectangles
▸ 1—13×21" rectangle
From brown wool, cut:
▸ 1 of Pattern A
From green plaid wool, cut:
▸ 1—⅜×8" strip for stem appliqué
▸ 1—⅜×6¾" strip for stem appliqué
▸ 1—⅜×6¼" strip for stem appliqué
▸ 1—⅜×5½" strip for stem appliqué
▸ 1—⅜×4¾" strip for stem appliqué
▸ 3 of Pattern D
From dark green wool, cut:
▸ 1 each of patterns E, E reversed, and F
From assorted wools in pink, purple, red, blue, yellow, and orange, cut:
▸ 3 each of patterns B and C
▸ 14 of Pattern G

appliqué pillow top

[1] Referring to **Appliqué Placement Diagram**, arrange appliqué shapes and 8"-long, 6¾"-long, 6¼"-long, 5½"-long, and 4¾"-long stems on tan homespun 13×21" appliqué foundation. Tuck ends of stems under basket and flower shapes. Baste or pin shapes in place.

[2] Using one strand of matching embroidery floss and working from bottom layer to top, whipstitch appliqués in place, except for G flowers.

[3] Using one strand of green floss and a running stitch, secure black seed beads through center of each leaf to make veins.

[4] Stitch four or five black seed beads to center of each G flower to secure in place.

[5] Stitch buttons to right-hand side of basket to complete pillow top.

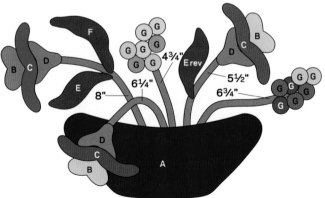

APPLIQUÉ PLACEMENT DIAGRAM

finish pillow

[1] With wrong side inside, fold each tan homespun 13×24" rectangle in half to make two 13×12" double-thick pillow back rectangles.

[2] Overlap folded edges of pillow back rectangles about 3" to make a 13×21" pillow back; baste around outer edges (see **Pillow Back Assembly Diagram**).

[3] Using ½" seam allowance, sew pillow back to pillow top around all edges to make pillow cover. Turn to right side and press. Insert pillow form through opening in pillow back.

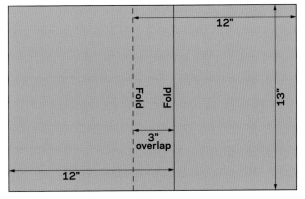

PILLOW BACK ASSEMBLY DIAGRAM

feathered
friends

A flock of appliquéd bluebirds and their chicks line up block by block in this fanciful, scrap-savvy wallhanging.

DESIGNER **KEVIN KOSBAB**   QUILT MAKER **JAN RAGALLER**   MACHINE QUILTER **KELLY EDWARDS**   PHOTOGRAPHER **ADAM ALBRIGHT**

materials

- 1¾ yards *total* assorted blue prints (bird body, wing appliqués, and binding)
- ⅛ yard solid orange (beak and feet appliqués)
- 1⅔ yards cream tone-on-tone print (appliqué foundations)
- 2½ yards backing fabric
- 42×51" batting
- Freezer paper
- Spray starch
- Fusible web
- Thread: Orange and black
- Clear monofilament polyester or nylon thread

Finished quilt: 36½×45½"
Finished blocks: 9" square

Quantities are for 44/45" -wide, 100% cotton fabrics. **Measurements** include ¼" seam allowances. Sew with right sides together unless otherwise stated.

cut fabrics

Cut pieces in the following order. Pattern pieces are on *Pattern Sheet 2*.

To make templates and prepare appliqué pieces A, B, E, and F, see Prepare Freezer-Paper Appliqués, *page 72*. To prepare appliqué pieces C, D, G, and H, see Prepare Fusible-Web Appliqués, *page 72*. (For more information, see Fusible-Web Method, *page 21*.)

From assorted blue prints, cut:
- 3 of Pattern A
- 2 of Pattern A reversed
- 18 of Pattern E
- 12 of Pattern E reversed
- 5 of Pattern B
- 30 of Pattern F
- Enough 2½"-wide strips to total 170" in length for binding

From solid orange, cut:
- 5 *each* of patterns C and D
- 30 *each* of patterns G and H

From cream tone-on-tone print, cut:
- 20—9½" squares

prepare freezer-paper appliqués

This project uses a freezer-paper-and-starch method for appliquéing the body (A and E) and wing (B and F) shapes. Instructions that follow are for this technique.

[1] Lay freezer paper, shiny side down, over patterns A, A reversed, B, E, E reversed, and F. Use a pencil to trace each pattern the number of times indicated in cutting instructions, leaving ½" between tracings.

[2] Place each sheet of drawn shapes, shiny side down, on a second sheet of freezer paper, also shiny side down. Fuse together with a hot, dry iron. Cut out layered shapes on drawn lines to make freezer-paper templates.

[3] Using a hot, dry iron, press a freezer-paper template, shiny side down, onto wrong side of designated fabric; let cool. Cut out fabric shape, adding a scant ¼" seam allowance to all edges (**Diagram 1**).

[4] Spray a small amount of spray starch into a dish or the cap of the starch bottle. Place a template-topped fabric

shape on pressing surface that is covered with a tea towel or muslin. Dip a small paintbrush or cotton swab into starch and moisten seam allowance of fabric shape (**Diagram 2**).

[5] Using the tip of a hot, dry iron, turn seam allowance over edge of freezer-paper template; press until fabric is dry. Press entire seam allowance, adding starch as necessary and ensuring fabric is pressed taut against template. At the point, fold fabric point over template point, then turn adjacent edges. Carefully peel off template to prepare appliqué shape.

[6] Repeat steps 3–5 to prepare remaining bird body and wing appliqués using fabrics indicated in cutting instructions.

prepare fusible-web appliqués

To use fusible web for appliquéing feet (C and G) and beak (D and H) shapes, complete following steps. (For more information on fusible-web appliqué, see Piece and Appliqué on *page 158*.)

[1] Lay fusible web, paper side up, over patterns. Use a pencil to trace each pattern the number of times indicated in cutting instructions, leaving ½" between tracings. Cut out each fusible-web shape roughly ¼" outside traced lines.

[2] Following the manufacturer's instructions, press fusible-web shapes onto wrong side of solid orange fabric; let cool. Cut out fabric shapes on drawn lines. Peel off paper backings to prepare appliqués.

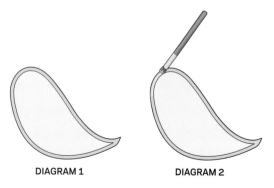

DIAGRAM 1   DIAGRAM 2

appliqué blocks

[1] Referring to **Diagram 3**, position blue print A body and solid orange C feet on a cream tone-on-tone print 9½" square. Pin feet in place; remove body appliqué.

[2] Following the manufacturer's directions, fuse feet in place. With orange thread and a short, narrow zigzag stitch, machine-appliqué feet.

[3] Reposition A body on cream tone-on-tone print square; pin. With clear monofilament thread and a blind-hem

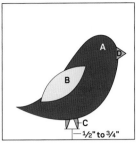

DIAGRAM 3

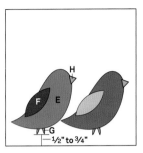

DIAGRAM 4

stitch, machine-appliqué body; to conceal backstitches, start and stop stitching where the wing will overlap the bird body. Referring to **Diagram 3**, position B wing on bird body; pin and stitch in place.

[4] Referring to Step 2, position, fuse, and stitch D beak to complete a mother bird A block.

[5] Using blue print A bird bodies and blue print B wings, repeat steps 1–4 to make three mother bird A blocks total.

[6] Position blue print A reversed body, blue print B wing, solid orange C feet, and solid orange D beak on a cream tone-on-tone print 9½" square in a mirror image of **Diagram 3**. Appliqué all pieces in place as before to make a mother bird B block. Repeat to make a second mother bird B block.

[7] Referring to **Diagram 4**, position two blue print E bodies, two blue print F wings, two solid orange G feet, and two solid orange H beaks on a cream tone-on-tone print 9½" square. Appliqué pieces as before to make a baby bird A block. Repeat to make nine baby bird A blocks total.

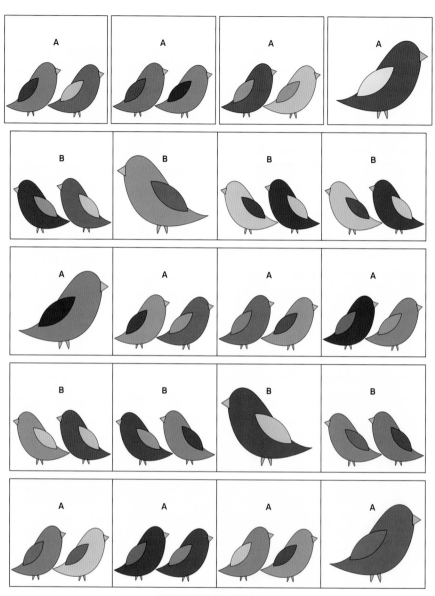

QUILT ASSEMBLY DIAGRAM

[8] Position two blue print E reversed bodies, two blue print F wings, two solid orange G feet, and two solid orange H beaks on a cream tone-on-tone print 9½" square in a mirror image of **Diagram 4** on *page 73*. Appliqué all pieces to make a baby bird B block. Repeat to make six baby bird B blocks total.

[9] Using black thread, machine-satin-stitch an eye on each bird (see photo on *page 73*). Start with a narrow stitch, increase the width, then narrow it again to make the eye round.

assemble quilt top

[1] Referring to **Quilt Assembly Diagram** for placement, lay out blocks in five rows. Sew together blocks in each row.

Press seams in one direction, alternating direction with each row.

[2] Join rows to make quilt top. Press seams in one direction.

finish quilt

[1] Layer quilt top, batting, and backing; baste. (For details, see Complete the Quilt, *page 159*.)

[2] Quilt as desired. The background of the featured quilt was machine-quilted with an allover swirl pattern. To mimic feathers, a wavelike design was machine-quilted in each wing.

[3] Bind with assorted blue print binding strips (for details, see Complete the Quilt).

color option

Chicken wire print fabric and 1940s feed sack reproductions combine for this cute wall hanging rendition of Feathered Friends. Each of the birds was machine blanket-stitched with black thread, then the three birds were accented with 1½"-, 1"-, and 3"-wide borders with fussy-cut farm print corners.

caramel & bubblegum

Make this big block quilt by cutting large circles from squares, then raw-edge appliqué the shapes to solid-color square backgrounds.

DESIGNER **JULIE HERMAN**   QUILT MAKER **JAN RAGALLER**   MACHINE QUILTER **LEANNE OLSON**   PHOTOGRAPHER **ADAM ALBRIGHT**

materials

- 2½ yards total assorted pink prints (blocks)
- 4¾ yards solid gray (blocks)
- ⅝ yard pink print (binding)
- 5⅛ yards backing fabric
- 73×92" batting

Finished quilt: 67×86"
Finished block: 9½" square

Quantities are for 44/45"-wide, 100% cotton fabrics. **Measurements** include ¼" seam allowances. Sew with right sides together unless otherwise stated.

cut fabrics

Cut pieces in the following order. Circle Pattern is on *Pattern Sheet 1*.

From assorted pink prints, cut:
- 32—10" squares

From solid gray, cut:
- 63—10" squares

From pink print, cut:
- 8—2½×42" binding strips

assemble blocks

[1] Fold a pink print 10" square in half vertically and horizontally to find center and divide square into quarters. Lightly finger-press to create positioning guidelines; unfold.

[2] Center Circle Pattern on wrong side of prepared assorted print square, and using a pencil, trace around circle. (To prevent fabric from stretching as you draw the line, place 220-grit sandpaper under the square.) Carefully cut out circle along drawn line, reserving square. Repeat to make 32 assorted pink print 6½" circles (you will use 31) and 32 assorted print 10" squares with a 6½"-diameter circle opening.

[3] Aligning raw edges, layer a pink print 10" square with a 6½"-diameter circle opening atop a solid gray 10" square (**Diagram 1**); pin. Sew pink print square to solid gray square ¼" from the circle's raw edge to make Block A; press. Designer Julie Herman recommends using a walking foot when sewing the curved piece to the foundation to prevent stretching the shape.

[4] Using assorted pink print 10" squares with a 6½"-diameter circle opening and solid gray 10" squares, repeat Step 3 to make 32 A blocks total.

[5] Fold a remaining solid gray 10" square in half vertically and horizontally; lightly finger-press to make positioning guidelines.

[6] Aligning positioning guidelines, center a pink print circle atop prepared solid gray square (**Diagram 2**); pin. Sew pink print circle to foundation ¼" from raw edge to make Block B. Press.

[7] Using assorted print circles and solid white 10" squares, repeat steps 5 and 6 to make 31 B blocks total.

[8] Fold an A block diagonally in both directions and lightly finger-press to make guidelines for quilting. Repeat with remaining A blocks and B blocks.

assemble quilt top

[1] Referring to **Quilt Assembly Diagram**, lay out blocks in nine rows, alternating A and B blocks.

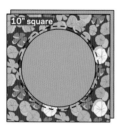

DIAGRAM 1

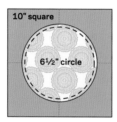

DIAGRAM 2

color option

If pink isn't your thing, try choosing a variety of colorful prints for the appliqués and using solid white for the block backgrounds. Seven different colors were chosen for this scrappy-look version, making it a great throw or blanket for just about any room of your home.

[2] Sew together blocks in each row, stitching through all three layers of fabric. Press seams toward B blocks.

[3] Join rows to complete quilt top. Press seams in one direction.

finish quilt

[1] Layer quilt top, batting, and backing; baste. (For details, see Complete the Quilt, *page 159*).

[2] Quilt as desired. The featured quilt was machine quilted with a floral motif inside each circle opening and on each circle appliqué. The block backgrounds feature petal-like stiched motifs.

[3] Bind with pink print binding strips. (For details, see Complete the Quilt.)

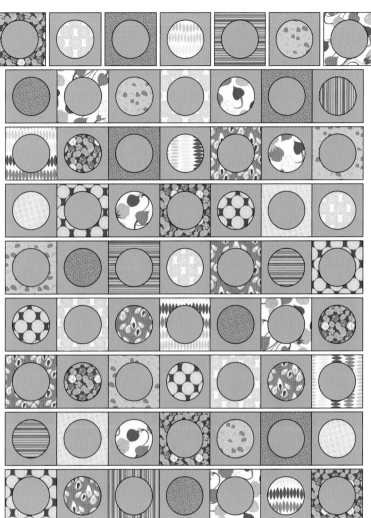

QUILT ASSEMBLY DIAGRAM

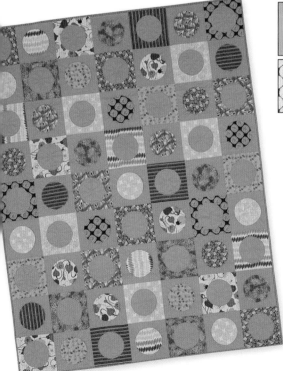

tip

Machine-wash and -dry the quilt to fray and soften raw edges of circular appliqué pieces.

intermediate

Enjoy the mix of shapes, layers, and dimensional
techniques among this collection of appliqué projects.

merry
go round

Fused-and-stitched appliqué pieces mix it up with patchwork in this tic-tac-toe meets pick-up-sticks wall hanging.

DESIGNER **LONNI ROSSI**   QUILT MAKER **MARY PEPPER**
MACHINE QUILTER **LEANNE OLSON**   PHOTOGRAPHER **ADAM ALBRIGHT**

materials

▸ 9—9×22" rectangles (fat eighths) assorted prints in gold-and-brown, light gold, gold, cream-and-green, gold-and-green, light green, green, green floral, and brown (quilt center)
▸ ¾ yard cream print (inner border)
▸ 1 yard yellow floral (outer border, binding)
▸ 2⅝ yards backing fabric
▸ 47" square batting
▸ Lightweight fusible web
▸ Clear monofilament thread

Finished quilt: 38½" square

Quantities are for 44/45"-wide, 100% cotton fabrics. **Measurements** include ¼" seam allowances. Sew with right sides together unless otherwise stated.

cut fabrics

Cut pieces in the following order. Appliqué patterns are on *Pattern Sheet 1.* To use fusible web for appliquéing, complete the following steps. (For more information, see Fusible-Web Method, *page 21.*)

[1] Lay fusible web, paper side up, over Pattern A. Use a pencil to trace the pattern nine times, leaving ½" between tracings. Cut out each fusible-web square roughly ¼" outside the traced line.

[2] Following the manufacturer's instructions, press fusible-web squares onto wrong side of designated fabrics; let cool.

tip

To produce uniform stitches when doing machine appliqué, work slowly and sew at an even pace. If possible, set your machine in the "needle down" position, and set the motor at half speed.

[3] Lay fusible web, paper side up, over Pattern B. Use a pencil to trace the pattern 17 times, leaving ½" between tracings. Cut out each fusible-web circle roughly ¼" outside the traced line.

[4] Following manufacturer's instructions, press fusible-web circles onto wrong side of designated fabrics; let cool.

[5] Lay fusible web, paper side up, over Strip Pattern A and Strip Pattern B. Use a pencil to trace each pattern nine times, leaving ½" between tracings. Cut out each pattern roughly ¼" outside the traced lines.

[6] Following the manufacturer's instructions, press fusible-web shapes onto designated fabrics; let cool.

[7] Carefully cut out all fabric shapes on drawn lines. The cut-out circles, squares, and ½"-wide strips are appliqués.

From each of nine assorted prints, you will cut one 4" A square, five ½×7" strips, and three ½×4" strips. From assorted prints, cut 17 B circles. Cut four of the B circles in half to make eight C half-circles total. Peel off paper backings.

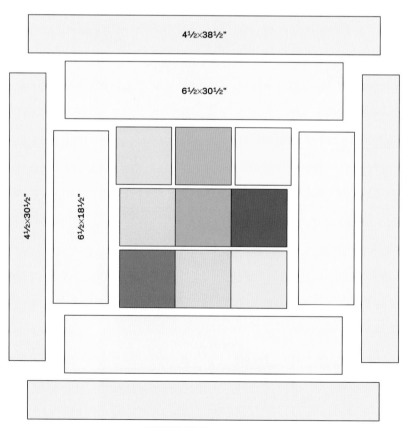

QUILT ASSEMBLY DIAGRAM

From each assorted print, cut:
- 1—6½" square
- 1 of Pattern A
- 1 of Pattern B (you will use a total of 17)
- 1 of Strip Pattern A
- 1 of Strip Pattern B

From cream print, cut:
- 2—6½×30½" inner border strips
- 2—6½×18½" inner border strips

From yellow floral, cut:
- 4—2½×42" binding strips
- 2—4½×38½" outer border strips
- 2—4½×30½" outer border strips

assemble quilt center

[1] Referring to **Quilt Assembly Diagram**, lay out nine assorted print 6½" squares in rows.

[2] Sew together pieces in each row. Press seams in one direction, alternating direction with each row.

[3] Join rows to make quilt center. Press seams in one direction. The quilt center should be 18½" square including seam allowances.

add borders

[1] Referring to **Quilt Assembly Diagram**, sew cream print 6½×18½" inner border strips to opposite edges of quilt center. Add cream print 6½×30½" inner border strips to remaining edges. Press all seams toward inner border.

[2] Join yellow floral 4½×30½" outer border strips to opposite edges of quilt center. Add yellow floral 4½×38½" outer border strips to remaining edges to complete quilt top. Press all seams toward outer border.

tip

If residue from fusible web, basting spray, or a glue stick builds up on your needle, wipe it off with a cotton ball dipped in rubbing alcohol.

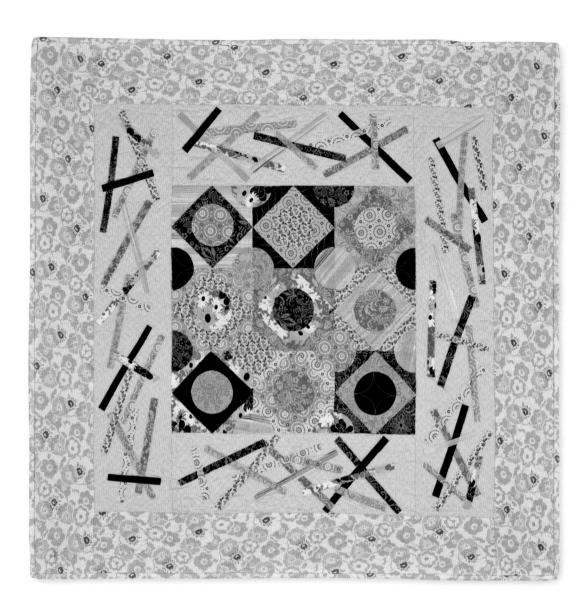

tip

Pivoting evenly around curves takes practice. Keep an eye on the space between your stitches as you work around the appliqué. Pivot often on a gentle rounded curve.

appliqué quilt

[1] Referring to **Appliqué Placement Diagram**, lay out appliqué pieces on quilt top. When you are pleased with the arrangement, fuse in place.

[2] Using clear monofilament thread, machine-zigzag-stitch around each appliqué.

finish quilt

[1] Layer quilt top, batting, and backing; baste. (For details, see Complete the Quilt, *page 159*.)

[2] Quilt as desired. This quilt was machine-quilted with an all-over feather design in the block backgrounds and outer border and a diamond pattern in the centers of the circle appliqués. Intersecting straight lines were used to quilt the inner border.

[3] Bind with yellow floral binding strips. (For details, see Complete the Quilt.)

APPLIQUÉ PLACEMENT DIAGRAM

color option

This pink version of Merry Go Round features a springlike fabric palette that's punched up with deep gold, charcoal, and magenta hues. The strip appliqués in the inner border point toward the quilt center.

To make an impressive, yet bare-bones version, omit the appliqués on the quilt center and inner border. Make the Nine-Patch quilt center from an assortment of fabrics that have strong light and dark contrast among them. Add complementary inner and outer borders.

zinniaflats

Spunky stripes and dots paired with dimensional appliqués give a contemporary quilt dazzling eye appeal.

DESIGNER **MARINDA STEWART**   PHOTOGRAPHER **GREG SCHEIDEMANN**

materials

- ▸ 1¼ yards aqua-and-white dot (appliqué foundations, blocks)
- ▸ ⅞ yard black-and-white stripe (stem appliqués, blocks, binding)
- ▸ ¾ yard red floral (flower appliqués, blocks)
- ▸ ¾ yard teal-and-red dot (blocks)
- ▸ ¼ yard black-and-white dot (leaf appliqués, sashing, flower ruffles)
- ▸ 1¼ yards red-white-and black floral (sashing)
- ▸ 18×22" piece (fat quarter) red-white-and black stripe (flower ruffles)
- ▸ 8" square white-and-red dot (yo-yos)
- ▸ ½ yard fusible web
- ▸ 3⅛ yards backing fabric
- ▸ 56" square batting

Finished quilt: 49½" square
Finished block: 20" square

Quantities are for 44/45"-wide, 100% cotton fabrics. **Measurements** include ¼" seam allowances. Sew with right sides together unless otherwise stated.

cut fabrics

Cut pieces in the following order. Patterns are on *Pattern Sheet 1*. To use fusible web for appliquéing pieces A, B, and C, complete the following steps. (For more information on fusible-web appliqué, see Fusible-Web Method, *page 21*.)

[1] Lay fusible web, paper side up, over patterns. Use a pencil to trace each pattern the number of times indicated in cutting instructions, leaving ½" between tracings. Cut out fusible-web shapes roughly ¼" outside traced lines.

[2] Following the manufacturer's instructions, press each fusible-web shape onto wrong side of designated fabric; let cool. Cut out fabric shapes on drawn lines; peel off paper backings.

From aqua-and-white dot, cut:
- ▸ 4—12½" squares
- ▸ 8—2⅛×18¾" strips
- ▸ 8—2⅛×15½" strips

From black-and-white stripe, cut:
- ▸ 6—2½×42" binding strips
- ▸ 8—1½×14½" strips
- ▸ 8—1½×12½" strips
- ▸ 4 of Pattern A

From red floral, cut:
- ▸ 8—1×15½" strips
- ▸ 8—1×14½" strips
- ▸ 4 of Pattern B

From teal-and-red dot, fussy-cut:
- ▸ 8—1⅜×20½" bias strips
- ▸ 8—1⅜×18¾" bias strips

From black-and-white dot, cut:
- 16 of Pattern C
- 9—3½" sashing squares
- 4—2½×11" strips

From red-white-and-black floral, fussy-cut:
- 12—3½×20½" sashing strips

From red-white-and-black stripe, cut:
- 4—2½×22" strips

From white-and-red dot, cut:
- 4 of Pattern D

appliqué block centers

[1] Referring to **Appliqué Placement Diagram**, lay out one A stem, one B flower, and four C leaves atop an aqua-and-white dot 12½" square. Fuse in place.

[2] Using thread to match appliqués and working from bottom layer to top, satin-stitch around each appliqué piece to make a block center.

[3] Repeat steps 1 and 2 to make four appliquéd block centers total.

assemble blocks

[1] Referring to **Block Assembly Diagram**, sew short black-and-white stripe strips to opposite edges of a block center. Join long black-and-white stripe strips to remaining edges. Press seams toward strips.

[2] Sew short red floral strips to opposite edges of block center. Join long red floral strips to remaining edges. Press seams toward strips. In the same manner, sew short aqua-and-white dot strips to opposite edges of block center. Join long aqua-and-white dot strips to remaining edges. Press seams toward strips.

[3] Sew short teal-and-red dot bias strips to opposite edges of block center, taking care not to stretch the bias strips. Join long teal-and-red dot strips to remaining edges to make a block. Press seams toward strips. The block should be 20½" square including seam allowances.

[4] Repeat steps 1–3 to make four blocks total.

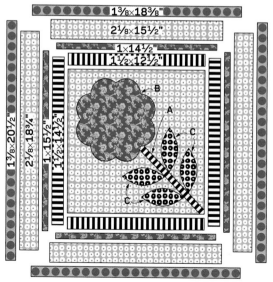

APPLIQUÉ PLACEMENT AND BLOCK ASSEMBLY DIAGRAM

QUILT ASSEMBLY DIAGRAM

assemble quilt top

[1] Referring to **Quilt Assembly Diagram**, lay out blocks, sashing strips, and sashing squares in five rows.

[2] Sew together pieces in each row. Press seams toward sashing strips.

[3] Join rows to complete quilt top. Press seams in one direction.

embellish flower appliqués

[1] With right sides together, join short edges of a red-white-and-black stripe 2½×22" strip to make a circle. Press seam open.

[2] Turn under ⅛" seam on one raw edge; topstitch in place.

[3] Using a running stitch, gather raw edge into a circle with a ½" opening; knot off to make a large ruffle (see photo, *page 80*).

[4] Repeat steps 1–3 to make four large ruffles total.

[5] Repeat Step 1 using a black-and-white dot 2½×11" strip to make a circle.

[6] Fold circle in half with wrong side inside. Clip raw edges at ¼" intervals.

[7] Using a running stitch, gather folded edge into a circle with a ½" opening; knot off to make a small ruffle (see photo).

[8] Repeat steps 5–7 to make four small ruffles total.

[9] Thread a needle with matching or neutral thread and tie a knot about 6" from end.

With a white-and-red dot D circle facedown, turn raw edge of circle a scant ⅛" toward circle center. Take small, evenly spaced running stitches near folded edge to secure it (**Diagram 1**). End stitching next to starting point. Do not cut thread. Gently pull thread ends to gather folded edge until it forms a circle (**Diagram 2**). Knot and trim thread to make a yo-yo. Repeat to make four yo-yos total.

[10] Layer a large ruffle, small ruffle, and yo-yo (see photo). Topstitch through all layers around outer edge of yo-yo to make a ruffle unit.

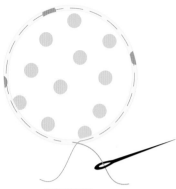

DIAGRAM 1

DIAGRAM 2

finish quilt

[1] Layer quilt top, batting, and backing; baste. (For details, see Complete the Quilt, *page 159*.)

[2] Quilt as desired. Designer Marinda Stewart used a long serpentine quilting stitch to fill the block backgrounds and the aqua-and-white dot strips. She then outline-quilted around each sashing strip. Marinda says the red-white-and-black floral sashing is a good place to practice your machine quilting by simply following the leaf and flower motifs. Center ruffle unit atop an appliquéd red floral flower and hand-stitch to secure. Repeat to embellish each flower.

[3] Bind with black-and-white stripe binding strips. (For details, see Complete the Quilt.)

budding
beauty

Bright 1930s print appliqués
make a cheery statement
on this yellow-and-white
bed-size quilt.

DESIGNER **LINDA HOHAG**
MACHINE QUILTER **JENISE ANTONY**
PHOTOGRAPHER **CAMERON SADEGHPOUR**

materials

- 1½ yards total assorted 1930s prints
  (bud appliqués)
- ⅓ yard solid green (stem appliqués)
- 4½ yards solid white (appliqué
  foundations, blocks)
- 2½ yards solid yellow (blocks, inner
  border)
- 1⅛ yards yellow print (blocks)
- 2½ yards green print (middle border,
  binding)
- 2¾ yards blue print (outer border)
- 8 yards backing fabric
- 95×110" batting
- Heat-resistant template plastic
- Liquid or spray starch
- Clear monofilament thread

Finished quilt: 88½×104"
Finished block: 11" square

Quantities are for 44/45"-wide, 100%
cotton fabrics. **Measurements** include
¼" seam allowances. Sew with right sides
together unless otherwise stated.

cut fabrics

Cut pieces in the following order. Cut inner
and outer border strips lengthwise (parallel
to selvage).

From assorted 1930s prints, cut:
- 320 of Bud Pattern (For details, see
  Prepare Appliqués, *page 94*.)

From solid green, cut:
- 80—¾×4" stem strips

From solid white, cut:
- 20—12" squares
- 5—9" squares, cutting each diagonally
  twice in an X for 20 large triangles total
  (you'll use 18)
- 60—4¾" squares, cutting each in half
  diagonally for 120 small triangles total

From solid yellow, cut:
- 2—1½×86" inner border strips
- 2—1½×72½" inner border strips
- 49—6⅜" squares, cutting each in half
  diagonally for 98 large triangles total

From yellow print, cut:
- 30—6" squares

From green print, cut:
- 9—2½×42" strips for middle border
- 10—2½×42" binding strips

From blue print, cut:
▸ 2—6½×92" outer border strips
▸ 2—6½×88½" outer border strips

prepare appliqués

The Bud Pattern is on *Pattern Sheet 4.* Designer Linda Hohag uses a starch method for appliquéing. (For more information, see Spray-Starch Method, *page 18.*) The instructions that follow are for this technique.

[1] Place heat-resistant template plastic over Bud Pattern. Using a pencil, trace pattern onto plastic (**Diagram 1**). Cut out on drawn lines to make a bud template.

[2] Place bud template on wrong side of a 1930s print fabric. Cut out bud appliqué piece, adding a ¼" seam allowance to edges (**Diagram 2**). If desired, trim across points to reduce bulk.

[3] Spray or pour a small amount of starch into a dish. Place template-topped fabric on a pressing surface covered with a tea towel or muslin. Dip a cotton swab in starch and moisten seam allowance of appliqué piece (**Diagram 3**).

[4] Use the tip of a hot, dry iron to turn seam allowance over edge of template; press it in place until fabric is dry (**Diagram 4**). Press entire seam allowance, adding starch as necessary and ensuring fabric is pressed taut against appliqué template.

[5] Turn template and appliqué piece over. Press appliqué from right side, then remove template.

[6] Repeat steps 2 through 5 to prepare each bud appliqué.

[7] Turn under a scant ¼" on each long edge of the solid green ¾×4" stem strips. Press, starching if desired.

appliqué blocks

[1] Fold each solid white 12" square in half diagonally twice. Lightly finger-press each fold to create 20 foundation squares with appliqué placement guidelines; unfold.

[2] Referring to **Appliqué Placement Diagram**, lay out four 4"-long stem appliqués and sixteen 1930s print buds on each solid white foundation square; pin or glue-baste in place.

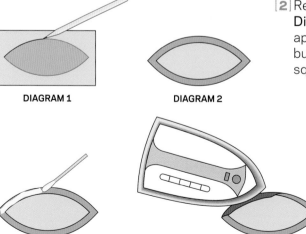

DIAGRAM 1

DIAGRAM 2

DIAGRAM 3

DIAGRAM 4

APPLIQUÉ PLACEMENT DIAGRAM

[3] Using clear monofilament thread and working from bottom layer to top, machine-zigzag-stitch around each appliqué to make 20 appliquéd blocks.

[4] Soak appliquéd blocks in cold water to remove starch. Machine-dry with dry towel to help absorb excess water. Trim excess foundation fabric from behind appliqués, leaving ¼" seam allowances. Press each block from wrong side and trim to 11½" square including seam allowances.

assemble square-in-a-square blocks and units

[1] Sew solid white small triangles to opposite edges of a yellow print 6" square (**Diagram 5**). Add solid white small triangles to remaining edges to make a Square-in-a-Square unit. Press all seams toward triangles. The unit should be 8¼" square including seam allowances. Repeat to make 30 Square-in-a-Square units total.

[2] Sew solid yellow large triangles to opposite edges of a Square-in-a-Square unit. Add solid yellow large triangles to remaining edges to make a Square-in-a-Square block (**Diagram 6**). Press all seams toward yellow triangles.

The block should be 11½" square including seam allowances. Repeat to make 12 Square-in-a-Square blocks total.

[3] Sew solid yellow large triangles to opposite edges of a Square-in-a-Square unit. Add a solid yellow large triangle to one remaining edge to make a side unit (**Diagram 7**). Press all seams toward yellow triangles. Repeat to make 14 side units total.

[4] Sew solid white large triangles to two solid yellow large triangles to make mirror-image triangle pairs. Press seams toward yellow triangles. Join triangle pairs to adjacent edges of a Square-in-a-Square unit to make a corner unit (**Diagram 8**). Repeat to make four corner units total.

assemble quilt center

[1] Referring to **Quilt Assembly Diagram**, lay out 20 appliquéd blocks, 12 Square-in-a-Square blocks, 14 side units, and 10 solid white large triangles in diagonal rows.

[2] Sew together pieces in each row. Press seams toward Square-in-a-Square blocks and side units.

tip

"Make multiple templates so you can starch several appliqués without waiting for the previous one to cool. With 320 buds to prepare, this small amount of time saved really adds up!"
—DESIGNER LINDA HOHAG

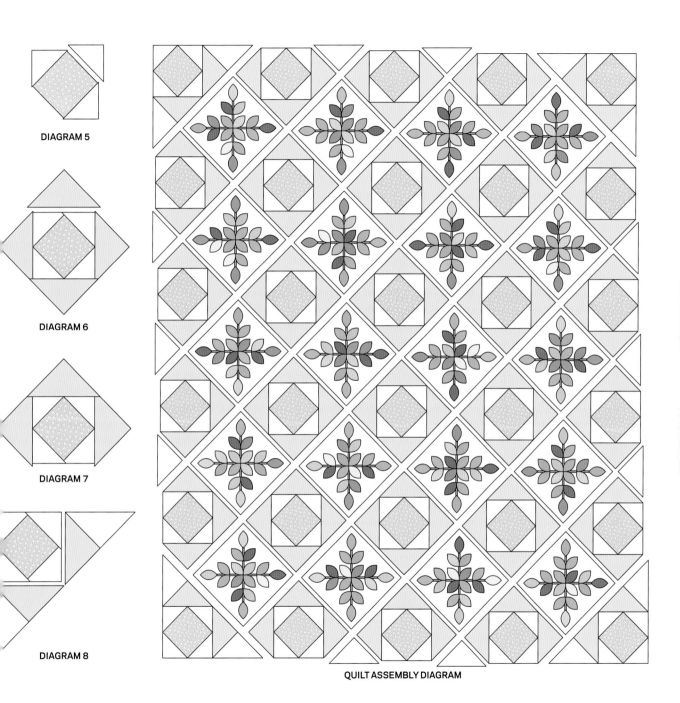

DIAGRAM 5

DIAGRAM 6

DIAGRAM 7

DIAGRAM 8

QUILT ASSEMBLY DIAGRAM

[3] Join rows; press seams in one direction. Add a corner unit to each corner to complete quilt center; press seams toward corner units. The quilt center should be 70½×86" including seam allowances.

add borders

[1] Sew long solid yellow inner border strips to long edges of quilt center. Join short inner border strips to remaining edges. Press all seams toward inner border.

[2] Cut and piece green print 2½×42" strips to make:
  ▸ 2—2½×88" middle border strips
  ▸ 2—2½×76½" middle border strips

[3] Sew long middle border strips to long edges of quilt center. Join short middle border strips to remaining edges. Press all seams toward middle border.

[4] Sew long blue print outer border strips to long edges of quilt center. Join short blue print outer border strips to remaining edges to complete quilt top. Press all seams toward outer border.

finish quilt

[1] Layer quilt top, batting, and backing. (For details, see Complete the Quilt, *page 159*.)

QUILTING DIAGRAM

[2] Quilt as desired. The featured quilt has a floral design machine-quilted in each Square-in-a-Square unit and a second floral design in each solid yellow and solid white large triangle (**Quilting Diagram**). The background of each appliquéd block features stippling and the borders are stitched in the ditch. A chain design was stitched in the middle border and a feather design in the outer border.

[3] Bind with green print binding strips. (For details, see Complete the Quilt.)

tip

To make a sharp point on each bud appliqué, moisten the seam allowance and fold the fabric point straight back over the point of the template. Push an adjacent edge of the seam allowance over the template edge. Repeat with remaining seam allowance.

stitching slowed down

If you'd like your project to be more portable, try hand appliqué. Prepare appliqué pieces in the same manner and baste or pin them to the appliqué foundation. Thread a sharps, betweens, straw, or milliner's needle with an 18" length of 100% cotton or silk, 50-weight thread in a color that matches the appliqué pieces. Strive for evenly spaced stitches that are barely visible on each appliqué piece, beginning and ending with a knot or a few backstitches.

dancing dots

Hard lines and soft curves make perfect partners when stitched together. Try your hand at using plastic templates and spray starch for a flawless performance.

DESIGNER **NANCY MAHONEY**   MACHINE QUILTER **KELLY WISE**   PHOTOGRAPHER **ADAM ALBRIGHT**

materials

- 1⅝ yards brown tone-on-tone (blocks A and B, binding)
- ¾ yard each of white-and-brown, white-and-green, and green-and-white prints (block A)
- 1⅛ yards each of orange dot and brown dot (appliqués)
- ⅞ yard multicolor floral (block B)
- ¾ yard red tone-on-tone (block B, inner border)
- ⅜ yard green tone-on-tone (block B)
- 1⅛ yards light green dot (block B)
- 1 yard orange floral (outer border)
- 4⅞ yards backing fabric
- 76×86" batting
- Heat-resistant template plastic
- Spray starch
- Clear monofilament thread

Finished quilt: 69½×79½"
Finished block: 10" square

Quantities are for 44/45"-wide, 100% cotton fabrics. **Measurements** include ¼" seam allowances. Sew with right sides together unless otherwise stated.

cut fabrics

Cut pieces in the following order.

Patterns are on *Pattern Sheet 4.* Designer Nancy Mahoney used a template-plastic-and-starch method to prepare appliqués. Instructions that follow are for this technique; see Prepare Appliqués, *page 102,* before cutting out appliqué pieces A and B.

From brown tone-on-tone, cut:
- 8—2½×42" binding strips
- 21—5⅞" squares, cutting each in half diagonally for 42 triangles total
- 21 of Pattern B

From *each* of white-and brown print, white-and-green print, and green-and-white print, cut:
- 21—5⅞" squares, cutting each in half diagonally for 42 triangles total

From each of orange dot and brown dot, cut:
- 42 of Pattern A

From multicolor floral, cut:
- 3—3×42" strips
- 42—3×5½" rectangles

From red tone-on-tone, cut:
- 3—3×42" strips
- 7—2×42" strips for inner border

From green tone-on-tone, cut:
▸ 21 of Pattern B
From light green dot, cut:
▸ 42—5½" squares
From orange floral , cut:
▸ 7—3½×42" strips for outer border
▸ 4—5" squares

prepare appliqués

[1] Lay heat-resistant template plastic over patterns A and B. Trace each pattern once onto plastic. Cut out shapes on drawn lines, making sure to include the ¼" seam allowance at ends of Pattern A, to make templates.

[2] Place a template right side down on wrong side of fabric indicated in cutting instructions and trace. Cut out appliqué shape, adding a scant ¼" seam allowance to curved edges.

[3] Spray a small amount of starch into a dish. Place template-topped appliqué piece on a pressing surface covered with a tea towel or muslin. Dip a cotton swab in starch and moisten seam allowance of appliqué piece (**Diagram 1**).

[4] Using the tip of a hot, dry iron, turn seam allowance over edge of template and press until fabric is dry. Press entire curved seam allowances in the same manner, adding starch as necessary and ensuring fabric is pressed taut against template.

For A arcs, clip inner curve as necessary and do not press under seam allowances on ends.

For B circles, you may wish to hand-stitch small running stitches ⅛" from the edges and pull them up to gather the fabric around the template before starching; this helps to evenly distribute the bulk.

[5] Turn the appliqué over and press it from the right side; remove template.

[6] Repeat steps 2–5 to cut and prepare the number of appliqué pieces indicated in cutting instructions.

assemble A blocks

[1] Sew together a white-and-brown print triangle and a brown tone-on-tone triangle to make a brown triangle-square (**Diagram 2**). Press seam toward brown tone-on-tone. The triangle-square should be 5½" square including seam allowances. Repeat to make 42 brown triangle-squares total.

DIAGRAM 1

DIAGRAM 2

tip

To highlight the edges of the arc and circle appliqués, use a decorative machine stitch and contrasting thread so the stitching stands out rather than blends in.

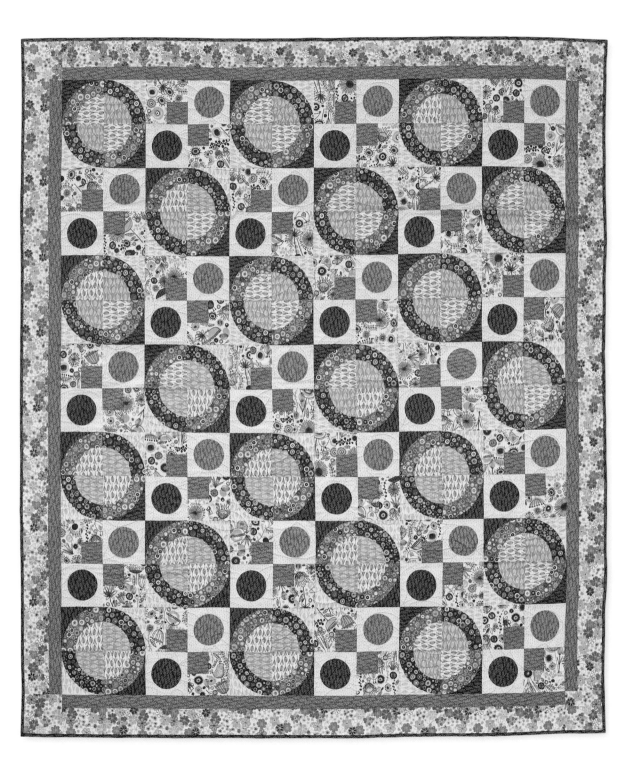

[2] Using white-and-green print triangles and green-and-white print triangles, repeat Step 1 to make 42 green triangle-squares (**Diagram 3**).

[3] Position a prepared orange dot A arc appliqué atop a brown triangle-square, aligning raw ends of arc with raw edges of triangle-square (**Diagram 4**). Baste or pin in place. Using clear monofilament thread and a narrow blind-hem stitch, sew along both curved edges to make an orange arc unit. Trim away excess fabric behind appliqué, leaving a ¼" seam allowance. Repeat to make 42 orange arc units total.

[4] Using prepared brown dot arc appliqués and green triangle-squares, repeat Step 3 to make 42 brown arc units (**Diagram 5**).

[5] Referring to **Diagram 6**, sew together two orange arc units and two brown arc units in pairs. Press seams in opposite directions. Join pairs to make block A.

Press seam in one direction. Block A should be 10½" square including seam allowances. Repeat to make 21 A blocks total.

assemble B blocks

[1] Sew together a red tone-on-tone 3×42" strip and a multicolor floral 3×42" strip to make a strip set (**Diagram 7**). Press seam toward red strip. Repeat to make three strip sets total. Cut strip sets into 42—3"-wide segments.

[2] Sew together a 3"-wide segment and a multicolor floral 3×5½" rectangle to make a three-patch unit (**Diagram 8**). Press seam toward rectangle. The unit should be 5½" square including seam allowances. Repeat to make 42 three-patch units total.

[3] Center a prepared green tone-on-tone B circle appliqué on a light green dot 5½" square; baste or pin in place (**Diagram 9**). Using clear monofilament

better blind-hem stitch

- A blind-hem stitch takes several straight stitches forward, one zigzag stitch, several more straight stitches, and another zigzag stitch. The straight stitches should pierce the foundation fabric right alongside the appliqué, and the zigzag stitches should just catch the appliqué edges.
- Use a size 60/8 embroidery needle in the machine, clear monofilament thread for the needle, and 60-weight thread in the bobbin.
- Set up your machine for a narrow (1 millimeter), short (1 millimeter) stitch.

BLIND-HEM STITCH

DIAGRAM 3

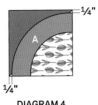

1/4"

1/4"

A

DIAGRAM 4

DIAGRAM 5

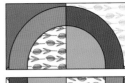

DIAGRAM 6

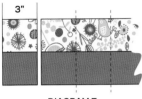

3"

DIAGRAM 7

DIAGRAM 8

B

DIAGRAM 9

thread and a narrow blind-hem stitch, sew around appliqué edges to make a green circle unit. Repeat to make 21 green circle units total.

[4] Using prepared brown tone-on-tone B circle appliqués, repeat Step 3 to make 21 brown circle units.

color option

Turn down the contrast of Dancing Dots by working with hand-dyed batiks. This throw-size version utilizes 24 different batiks in four distinct colorways. By reserving certain colorways for various appliqués and planning the positioning of the colors, the quilt comes together with a harmonious look.

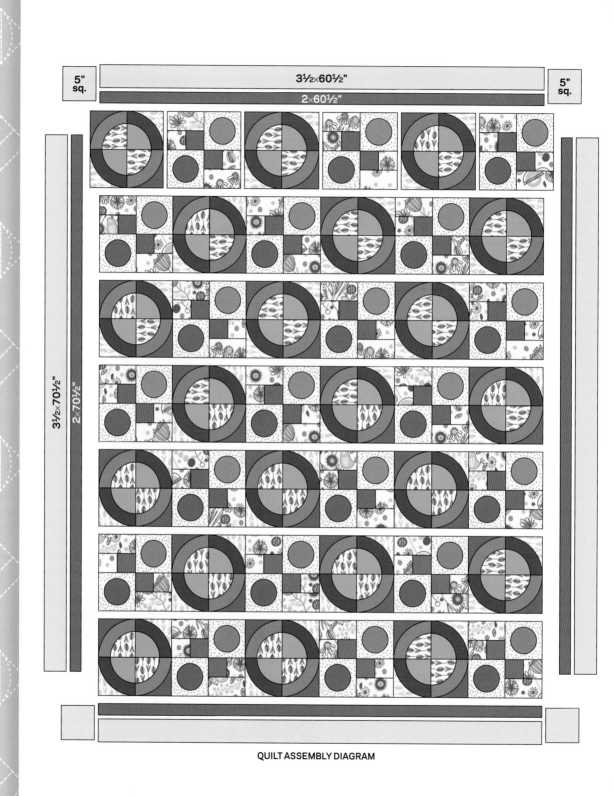

QUILT ASSEMBLY DIAGRAM

[5] Referring to **Diagram 10**, sew together two three-patch units, a green circle unit, and a brown circle unit in pairs. Press seams in opposite directions. Join pairs to make block B. Press seam in one direction. Block B should be 10½" square including seam allowances. Repeat to make 21 B blocks total.

assemble quilt top

[1] Referring to **Quilt Assembly Diagram**, lay out blocks in seven rows, alternating A and B blocks. Sew together blocks in each row. Press seams toward B blocks.

[2] Join rows to make quilt center. Press seams in one direction. The quilt center should be 60½×70½" including seam allowances.

[3] Cut and piece red tone-on-tone 2×42" strips to make:
   ▸ 2—2×70½" inner border strips
   ▸ 2—2×60½" inner border strips

[4] Cut and piece orange floral 3½×42" strips to make:
   ▸ 2—3½×70½" outer border strips
   ▸ 2—3½×60½" outer border strips

[5] Join a long inner border strip and a long outer border strip to make a long border unit. Press seam toward inner border strip. Repeat to make a second long border unit. Sew long border units to long edges of quilt center. Press seams toward border units.

[6] Sew together a short inner border strip and a short outer border strip; press seam toward inner border strip.

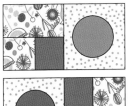
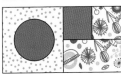

DIAGRAM 10

QUILTING DIAGRAM

Add orange floral 5" squares to ends of joined strips to make a short border unit. Press seams toward squares. Repeat to make a second short border unit.

[7] Sew short border units to remaining edges of quilt center to complete quilt top. Press seams toward border units.

finish quilt

[1] Layer quilt top, batting, and backing; baste. (For details, see Complete the Quilt, *page 159*.)

[2] Quilt as desired. This featured quilt was machine-quilted with leaf and loop motifs across the quilt top (**Quilting Diagram**).

[3] Bind with brown tone-on-tone binding strips. (For details, see Complete the Quilt.)

sew your seeds

Using a bit of hand appliqué and beading, transform scraps of cotton, wool, and velvet into a funky floral needle keeper.

DESIGNER **SUE SPARGO**   PHOTOGRAPHER **MARTY BALDWIN**

materials

- 3×12" piece multicolor floral (appliqué base)
- 7×12" piece eggplant felted wool (cover)
- Scraps of yellow, royal blue, orange, pink, and aqua felted wool (flower appliqués)
- Scraps of blue and pink florals (flower appliqués)
- Scraps of green velvet (leaf appliqués)
- 4×7" piece green felted wool (grass appliqués)
- 9×22" piece (fat eighth) blue print (lining)
- 6×13" piece fuchsia felted wool (pages)
- 7×12" thin cotton batting
- Thread: wool and cotton, in colors that match appliqués and beads
- 17 small heishi beads (flat, sequin-like beads): red
- Seed beads: yellow, green, and purple
- Scraps of yarn: green, yellow, orange, aqua, and pink
- ¼ yard baby rickrack: yellow
- Freezer paper
- ¼" hole punch (optional)
- Pinking shears or rotary cutter with wavy blade
- Straw needles: Nos. 11 and 10
- Chenille needles: Nos. 24 and 18

Finished needle case: 10½×6" open, 3½×6" closed

Fabrics are 100% cotton unless otherwise specified. **Measurements** include ¼" seam allowances. Sew with right sides together unless otherwise stated.

cut fabrics

Cut pieces in the following order. Patterns are on *Pattern Sheet 2.*

To felt your own wool, machine-wash it in a hot-water-wash, cool-rinse cycle with a small amount of detergent; machine-dry on high heat and steam-press.

To use freezer paper to prepare appliqué pieces, complete the following steps. (For more information, see Freezer-Paper Right-Side Method on *page 20.)*

[1] Lay freezer paper, shiny side down, over patterns. Use a pencil to trace each pattern the number of times indicated in cutting instructions, leaving ¼" between shapes. Cut out each freezer-paper shape on drawn lines.

[2] Using a hot, dry iron, press each freezer-paper shape, shiny side down, onto right side of designated cotton, wool, or velvet fabrics; let cool.

[3] Cut out cotton and velvet shapes, adding a ¼" seam allowance beyond drawn lines. Cut out wool shapes on drawn lines. (Felted wool doesn't fray, so there is no need to add seam allowances for turning under.) Peel off freezer paper.

From multicolor floral, cut:
▸ 1 of Pattern A

From eggplant wool, cut:
▸ 1—6½×11" rectangle

From yellow wool, cut:
▸ 13 of Pattern E (or use ¼" hole punch to punch thirteen ¼" wool circles)

From royal blue wool, cut:
▸ 7 of Pattern E (or use ¼" hole punch to punch seven ¼" wool circles)

From yellow, orange, pink, and aqua wool and blue and pink florals, cut:
▸ 1 each of patterns B, C, D, I, J, M, N, Q, and R
▸ 3 of Pattern K
▸ 2 of Pattern O

From green velvet, cut:
▸ 3 each of patterns F and G

From green wool, cut:
▸ 1 each of patterns H, L, and P

From blue print, cut:
▸ 1—6½×11" rectangle

From batting, cut:
▸ 1—6½×11" rectangle

From fuchsia wool, cut:
▸ 2—5½×6" rectangles, trimming each edge with pinking shears

APPLIQUÉ PLACEMENT DIAGRAM

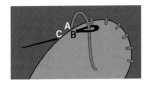

WHIPSTITCH DIAGRAM

HEISHI BEAD
STITCHING DIAGRAM

appliqué needle case front

[1] Position multicolor floral A appliqué base on bottom edge of eggplant wool 6½×11" rectangle (**Appliqué Placement Diagram**). Using matching thread and turning under ¼" seam allowance with your needle as you stitch, hand-appliqué scalloped edge in place; carefully clip seam allowance at each inner point in order to turn it under. Baste or pin remaining appliqué edges in place.

[2] Referring to **Appliqué Placement Diagram**, arrange all remaining appliqués except Q bird body and R bird wing on eggplant rectangle. Cut rickrack into three stems; position stems on eggplant rectangle, tucking ends under flower and grass pieces.

[3] Using threads that match appliqués, stitch around cotton and velvet shapes with Step 1 needle-turn technique.

(Designer Sue Spargo recommends using 60-weight cotton thread and a No. 10 or 11 straw needle.)

[4] Using threads that match appliqués, whipstitch wool shapes in place. (Sue used 12-weight, 50% wool/50% acrylic thread and a No. 24 chenille needle.)
To whipstitch, bring needle up at A and down at B (**Whipstitch Diagram**). Continue in same manner around entire appliqué shape.

add beading

[1] Referring to **Appliqué Placement Diagram**, arrange red heishi beads on H, L, and P grass pieces. Using red thread, bring needle up through center of bead and back into fabric at edge of bead. Continue in the same manner, sewing over bead four or eight times (**Heishi Bead Stitching Diagram**).

[2] Referring to photo on *page 110*, and **Appliqué Placement Diagram**, add yellow seed beads around D, I, and O flower pieces. (Sue used 60-weight cotton thread and a No. 11 straw needle.)

To add beads, bring needle up at A, the point where the first bead is desired (**Seed Bead Stitching Diagram**). Thread a seed bead onto needle, then insert the needle back into fabric at B, just to the right of A. Bring needle up at C, a bead's width to the left of A. Continue in same manner to outline shape with beads; after every fifth bead, take a tiny backstitch to anchor.

[3] Referring to photo opposite and **Appliqué Placement Diagram**, add green seed beads in pairs through center of F and G leaves.

add couching

[1] To couch around appliqués, thread yarn onto No. 18 chenille needle. Bring needle up where you want couching to begin and lay yarn down in shape's

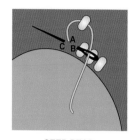

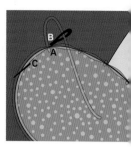

SEED BEAD STITCHING DIAGRAM

COUCHING DIAGRAM

outline. With a strand of cotton or wool thread and a smaller needle, stitch over yarn, making sure stitches are uniform (**Couching Diagram**). At end of couched line, bring tail end of yarn to the back. With small stitches, sew yarn tail to back of fabric, stitching only partway through wool so stitches do not show on front.

[2] Couch green yarn around each grass shape. Referring to photo on *page 110*, couch yellow yarn around left-hand flower, orange yarn around center flower, and aqua and pink yarns around right-hand flower.

color option

Cotton prints mixed with wools, delicate beads, and a careful choice of threads give this fusible-appliqué version of Sew Your Seeds a vintage flair. By stitching around the appliqués with matching thread, the flowers take on a romantic, traditional look.

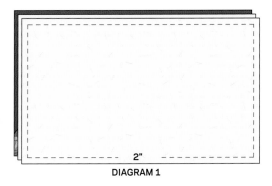

DIAGRAM 1

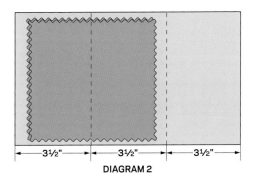

DIAGRAM 2

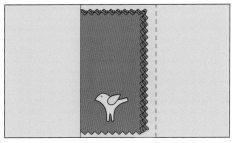

DIAGRAM 3

BIRD APPLIQUÉ DIAGRAM

assemble needle case

[1] Layer appliquéd and embellished eggplant wool rectangle and blue print lining rectangle with right sides together. Place batting rectangle on top. Sew around all edges, leaving a 2" opening for turning (**Diagram 1**).

[2] Clip corners and turn needle case right side out. Hand-sew opening closed.

[3] Layer fuchsia wool 5½×6" pages and position them on lining side of needle case so their center is 3½" from left-hand edge of needle case (**Diagram 2**). Machine-straight-stitch through center of fuchsia rectangles. Then stitch 3½" from right-hand edge of needle case.

[4] Fold fuchsia wool pages in half on stitched line (**Diagram 3**). Appliqué Q bird and R wing in place on first page (**Bird Appliqué Diagram**). Add a purple seed bead for the bird's eye to complete needle case.

RIGHT *Inside view: Four wool "pages" hold needles and pins for appliqué on the go. An appliquéd bird motif is just for fun.*

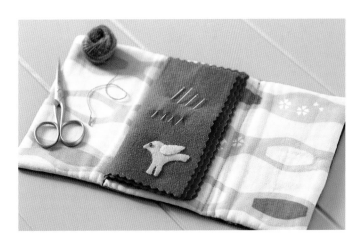

wool blooms

With felted wool for both foundation and appliqué, texture abounds on this luscious pillow.

DESIGNER **RENÉE NANNEMAN**   PHOTOGRAPHER **GREG SCHEIDEMANN**

materials

- ▸ ⅔ yard 54"-wide black-and-brown-check wool (pillow top, back, piping)
- ▸ 6×9" piece brown felted wool (basket appliqué)
- ▸ Scraps of assorted felted wool (listed in order from light to dark): beige, light pink, pink, deep rose, red, burgundy, and brick red (flower appliqués)
- ▸ Scraps of assorted green felted wool (leaf appliqués)
- ▸ ½ yard flannel (interlining)
- ▸ 16 assorted ¾"- to 1¼"-diameter shell buttons
- ▸ Perle cotton No. 5: light green
- ▸ 2⅛ yards of ¼"-diameter cord
- ▸ Freezer paper
- ▸ Polyester fiberfill
- ▸ Tacky glue

Finished pillow: 19½×17"

Measurements include ¼" seam allowances. Sew with right sides together unless otherwise stated.

cut fabrics

Cut pieces in the order that follows.

To felt the black-and-brown-check wool, machine-wash it in a warm-water-wash, cold-rinse cycle. Machine-dry it on high heat and remove promptly.

Patterns are on *Pattern Sheet 3*. To use freezer paper for cutting appliqué shapes, complete the following steps.

[1] Lay freezer paper, shiny side down, over patterns. Use a pencil to trace each pattern the number of times indicated in cutting instructions, leaving ½" between tracings. Cut out freezer-paper shapes roughly ¼" outside the traced lines.

tip

To felt wool, designer Renée Nanneman machine-washes it in a warm-wash/cold-rinse cycle and always dries it with a fabric softener sheet. She's found that one yard of 54"-wide wool will shrink up to a soft and fluffy piece approximately 32×52".

[2] Using a hot, dry iron, press freezer-paper shapes, shiny side down, onto right side of designated fabrics; let cool. Cut out fabric shapes on drawn lines and peel off freezer paper.

From black-and-brown-check wool, cut:
▸ 2—2¼×40" strips
▸ 2—20×17½" rectangles
From brown wool, cut:
▸ 1 of Pattern A
From beige wool scraps, cut:
▸ 1 *each* of patterns Q and DD
From light pink wool scraps, cut:
▸ 1 *each* of patterns J and V
From pink wool scraps, cut:
▸ 1 *each* of patterns C, D, G, K, L, R, AA, CC, EE, and GG
From deep rose wool scraps, cut:
▸ 1 *each* of patterns E, H, O, U, X, and BB
From red wool scraps, cut:
▸ 1 *each* of patterns F, I, P, M, W, Y, Z, and FF
From burgundy wool scraps, cut:
▸ 1 *each* of patterns B, N, and S
From brick red wool scraps, cut:
▸ 1 of pattern T
From green wool scraps, cut:
▸ 1 *each* of patterns HH, II, JJ, KK, LL, MM, and NN
From flannel, cut:
▸ 2—20×17½" rectangles

appliqué pillow top

[1] Center and chalk-mark a 16×13½" placement rectangle (2" from each edge) on a black-and-brown-check wool 20×17½" rectangle.

[2] Center brown wool A basket along the bottom chalk-marked line. Referring to **Appliqué Placement Diagram**, position flower, flower center, and leaf appliqués, keeping pieces within the chalked rectangle.

[3] Using thread to match each appliqué, whipstitch each flower center to its corresponding flower. Then, using small dots of tacky glue, lightly glue-baste basket, flowers, and leaves in place.

[4] Using thread to match each appliqué and working from bottom layer to top, whipstitch the layered flowers and leaves in place.

[5] Use light green perle cotton to sew buttons to each flower center with a French knot in each button's holes.
To make a French knot, bring your needle up through one hole of the button. Wrap the trailing perle cotton around the needle four to six times (**French Knot Diagram**). Insert the tip of the needle back through the hole of the button and into the wool, gently pushing the wraps down the needle to meet the button. Pull the needle and trailing perle cotton through the layers of wool slowly and smoothly, using needle-nose pliers if necessary.

[6] Place appliquéd rectangle right side down on a flat surface. Place a flannel 20×17½" rectangle on top; machine-baste ⅛" from all edges to make pillow top.

prepare piping

[1] Piece black-and-brown-check wool 2¼×40" strips to make one long 2¼"-wide piping strip.

[2] Wrong sides together, fold strip in half lengthwise. Insert cording next to

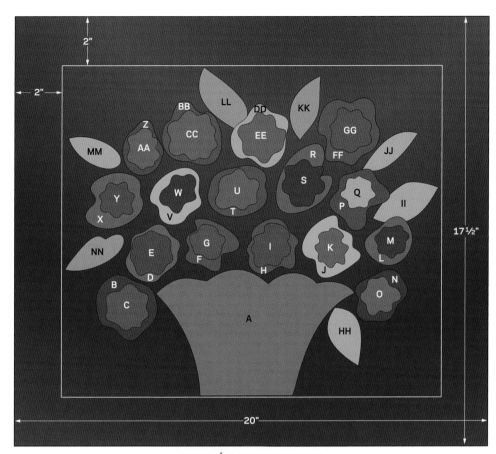

APPLIQUÉ PLACEMENT DIAGRAM

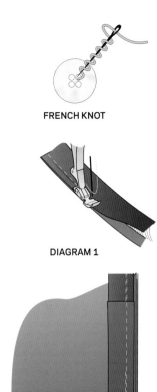

FRENCH KNOT

DIAGRAM 1

DIAGRAM 2

folded edge with cording end 1" from strip's end. With a zipper foot, baste through fabric layers right next to cording to make piping (**Diagram 1**).

assemble pillow

[**1**] Layer remaining black-and-brown-check 20×17½" rectangle and flannel 20×17½" rectangle; machine-baste ⅛" from all edges to make pillow back.

[**2**] Aligning raw edges, baste piping to all edges of pillow top, starting 2" from

piping end. As you stitch each corner, clip seam allowance to within a few threads of stitching line (**Diagram 2**); gently ease piping in place. Cut end of cording to abut snugly with beginning of piping, then trim excess wool strip about 1" longer. Overlap the extra 1" of wool strip around beginning of piping, then stitch to beginning point.

[**3**] Join pillow back to pillow top, stitching around all edges and leaving an opening for turning. Turn right side out, stuff with fiberfill, and stitch the opening closed.

out on a limb

One scroll-shape wool appliqué—turned, cut, stretched, and flipped—creates a stylized tree for a colorful bird with embroidered feathers.

DESIGNER **JANET CARIJA BRANDT**   PHOTOGRAPHER **GREG SCHEIDEMANN**

materials

Note: Before beginning, read "Free-Motion Embroidery Made Easy," page 125, for techniques and supplies to make the embroidery steps go smoothly.

- 1¾ yards 58/60"-wide cream felted wool (appliqué foundation)
- 1 yard 58/60"-wide red felted wool (appliqués)
- ½ yard red-and-white dot (binding)
- 3¼ yards backing fabric
- 58×67" batting
- Rayon machine-embroidery thread: red, yellow, blue, and green
- 50-weight cotton bobbin thread
- Temporary fabric adhesive
- Freezer paper
- Air-soluble marker
- 18" square of lightweight tear-away stabilizer

Finished quilt: 52×61"

Quantities are for 44/45"-wide, 100% cotton fabrics unless otherwise indicated. **Measurements** include ¼" seam allowances. Sew with right sides together unless otherwise stated.

cut fabrics

Cut pieces in the following order.

To felt wool, machine-wash it in a hot-water-wash, cold-rinse cycle. Machine-dry it on high heat and steam-press.

Patterns are on *Pattern Sheet 3.* To use freezer paper for cutting appliqué shapes, complete the following steps. (For more information, see Freezer-Paper Right-Side Method on *page 20.)*

[1] Lay freezer paper, shiny side down, over patterns. Use a pencil to trace each pattern the number of times indicated in cutting instructions, leaving ½" between tracings. Cut out freezer-paper shapes roughly ¼" outside traced lines. (Designer Janet Carija Brandt recommends reusing each freezer-paper shape a couple of times.)

[2] Using a hot, dry iron, press freezer-paper shapes, shiny sides down, onto right side of red wool; let cool. Cut out wool shapes on drawn lines and peel off freezer paper.

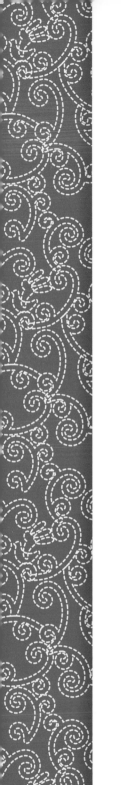

From cream wool, cut:
▸ 1—52×61" rectangle
From red wool, cut:
▸ 6 each of patterns B and B reversed
▸ 4 of Pattern C
▸ 1 each of patterns A, D, and E
▸ 3 of Pattern F
From red-and-white dot, cut:
▸ 6—2½×42" binding strips

appliqué quilt top

[1] On a design wall or large worktable, spread out cream wool 52×61" appliqué foundation.

[2] On appliqué foundation, arrange red wool A trunk and red wool B, B reversed, and C branches as desired to create a tree design. Use photo on *page 119* and **Appliqué Placement Diagram** as guides.

"Because of the stretchy nature of wool, it is unlikely any two of these quilts will be identical," Janet says. Ease some of the wool branches into more curvy shapes, if desired, and mark any branches you want to shorten; do not trim them until Step 4.

[3] Position D, E, and F bird pieces together on a branch, adjusting branch positions if necessary.

[4] When you're pleased with the arrangement, remove one piece at a time and spray the back with temporary adhesive. Reposition piece on appliqué foundation. Where branches overlap, trim so pieces butt together snugly.

[5] Using red thread and working from bottom layer to top, machine-blanket-stitch around each appliqué to complete quilt top.

color option

The branch patterns transform into a wrought-iron gate with a bright background in this rendition of Out on a Limb. To get this look, fuse solid black appliqués to a single piece of fabric, then trim the quilt center to 38×24" after the pieces are appliquéd. Then add three borders in finished widths of ½", 1¼", and 3", respectively.

APPLIQUÉ PLACEMENT DIAGRAM

embellish quilt top

Refer to the following steps to embroider bird on the quilt top. For more tips on the technique, see opposite.

[1] The full-size Embroidery Placement Diagram is on *Pattern Sheet 3*. Referring to Embroidery Placement Diagram, use air-soluble marker to draw main areas of design (**Photo 1**, *opposite*). If embroidery space on your quilt differs from that in the photo, draw elements that fit and add or subtract scrolls, curls, and leaves as desired.

[2] Spray tear-away stabilizer with temporary adhesive and place it on back of appliqué foundation where you plan to embroider.

[3] Set up your machine for free-motion stitching according to your machine's manual. Generally, you lower the feed dogs and attach a free-motion, embroidery, or hopper foot. Thread needle with 40-weight rayon or polyester embroidery thread and use 50-weight cotton bobbin thread in the bobbin.

[4] Using red machine-embroidery thread and a straight stitch, sew on drawn lines (**Photo 2**).

[5] Using machine-embroidery threads in a variety of colors, sew over first stitching lines as desired. Then use a straight stitch or decorative stitches to fill in desired areas (**Photo 3**).

[6] Using blue machine-embroidery thread, outline any desired areas by stitching over sewn lines again (**Photo 4**).

finish quilt

[1] Layer quilt top, batting, and backing; baste. (For details, see Complete the Quilt, *page 159*.)

[2] Quilt as desired. The cream background of the featured quilt was machine-quilted with an all over stipple using matching thread.

[3] Bind with red-and-white dot binding strips. (For details, see Complete the Quilt.)

designer notes

Big, bold, contemporary designs motivated Janet Carija Brandt to try a similar look in wool. "People think of wool as being muted and countrylike," she says, "but it can be anything you want."

To create the tree, Janet cut multiple whole branches (Pattern B), then combined them into a tree shape she liked, cutting off scrolls if necessary (which created Pattern C). Follow her lead to improvisationally mix branches.

free-motion embroidery made easy

1. Spray appliqué pieces with temporary fabric adhesive to hold them in place without pins. Designer Janet Carija Brandt prefers 505 Spray and Fix; it's low-tack and won't gum up your sewing machine needle.

2. Back the area you're going to stitch with tear-away stabilizer to prevent puckers and have greater control.

3. Draw a few lines and shapes on layered wool and tear-away stabilizer scraps to practice stitching before beginning work on your project.

4. Stitch with your hands flat on either side of the embroidery area. Gently move the fabric in any direction to straight-stitch on the drawn lines.

5. Relax! Remember, there are no mistakes, just extra stitches. To reinforce the design's shapes, stitch over lines more than once in matching or contrasting thread.

6. Consider that freehand embroidery need not be totally freehand. Draw as many lines as you like, perhaps adding new lines each time you change colors. This will make the process less intimidating.

7. Work in stages, one color at a time.

8. Repeat colors. You can always add more color. The more stitches in an area, the more intense the color.

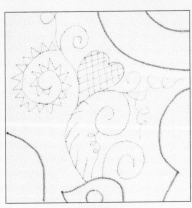

PHOTO 1

PHOTO 2

PHOTO 3

PHOTO 4

sunflower
trio

Use a 3-D fabric-folding technique to make stunning Sunburst blocks with ease—and with perfect points.

DESIGNER **EDYTA SITAR**   PHOTOGRAPHER **GREG SCHEIDEMANN**

materials

- ⅔ yard raspberry batik (petals in blocks)
- ⅜ yard yellow-orange batik (points in blocks)
- ¼ yard green batik (circle appliqués)
- ⅜ yard gold batik (appliqué foundations)
- ⅝ yard multicolor batik (setting triangles)
- ⅜ yard dark purple batik (binding)
- 1⅝ yards backing fabric
- 24×58" batting
- Freezer paper
- Fabric glue stick

Finished table runner: 17½×51½"
Finished block: 12" square

Quantities are for 44/45"-wide, 100% cotton fabrics. **Measurements** include ¼" seam allowances. Sew with right sides together unless otherwise stated.

cut fabrics

Cut pieces in the following order. Patterns are on *Pattern Sheet 1*.

Make templates of patterns A and B. For details, see Make and Use Templates, *page 157*.

To use freezer paper for cutting Pattern C, complete the following steps.

[1] Lay freezer paper, shiny side down, over Pattern C. Use a pencil to trace pattern three times. Cut out each freezer-paper circle on drawn line.

[2] Place a dab of fabric glue on dull side of each freezer-paper circle, then place glue side down on wrong side of green batik. Cut out fabric pieces, adding a scant ¼" seam allowance to all edges.

[3] Using the tip of a hot, dry iron, turn fabric seam allowance over edge of each freezer-paper circle and press taut against template. Clip seam allowance if necessary.

From raspberry batik, cut:
- 96 of Pattern A

From yellow-orange batik, cut:
- 48 of Pattern B

From green batik, cut:
- 3 of Pattern C

From gold batik, cut:
- 3—12½" squares

From multicolor batik, cut:
▸ 1—18¼" square, cutting it diagonally twice in an X for 4 setting triangles total

From dark purple batik, cut:
▸ 4—2½×42" binding strips

assemble appliqués

[1] To indicate the seam line on top arcs of A pieces, cut off seam allowance from top arc of Pattern A template, then use this to mark stitching line on half of the raspberry batik A pieces (**Photo A**).

[2] Sew together a marked and an unmarked A piece around top arcs only, stitching on marked line. Trim seam allowances of arcs to ⅛" (**Photo B**).

[3] Turn joined A pieces right side out to make a petal (**Photo C**). Press, then trim the back A piece ¼" from bottom edge of arc (**Photo D**).

[4] Repeat steps 1 through 3 to make 48 petals total.

[5] Fold tip of each yellow-orange batik B triangle ¼" to wrong side (**Photo E**). Fold each triangle in half lengthwise with wrong side inside; finger-press (**Photo F**).

[6] Aligning raw right-hand edges, place a folded B triangle on right side of a petal.

Bottom points of pieces should meet and B triangle tip will extend beyond top edge. Lay a second petal on top of first petal, sandwiching yellow-orange batik piece inside (**Photo G**). Sew along edge through all layers to make a petal pair. From wrong side, finger-press seam open (**Photo H**).

[7] With right side up, place a petal pair on ironing board. Align pressed center line of B triangle with center seam of petal pair (**Photo I**). (Don't worry that the B triangle's lower edge will be more than ¼" from bottom edge of petals when pressed open—this will all be covered by a C circle appliqué.) Press with tip of iron, starting at open end of B triangle and stopping about 1" from tip. Finish pressing from wrong side to prevent B triangle from being flattened.

[8] Repeat steps 6 and 7 to make and press 24 petal pairs total.

[9] Lay out eight petal pairs in a circle. Join petal pairs to make quarter circles, adding a folded B triangle into seam as before. Sew together quarter circles into half circles, and join half circles to make a sunburst appliqué, adding a folded B triangle into each seam. Repeat to make three sunburst appliqués total.

tip

To mimic designer Edyta Sitar's style of machine appliqué, use a very small zigzag stitch, about 20 to 24 stitches per inch. The zigzag width should be just large enough to grab the background and the appliqué edge.

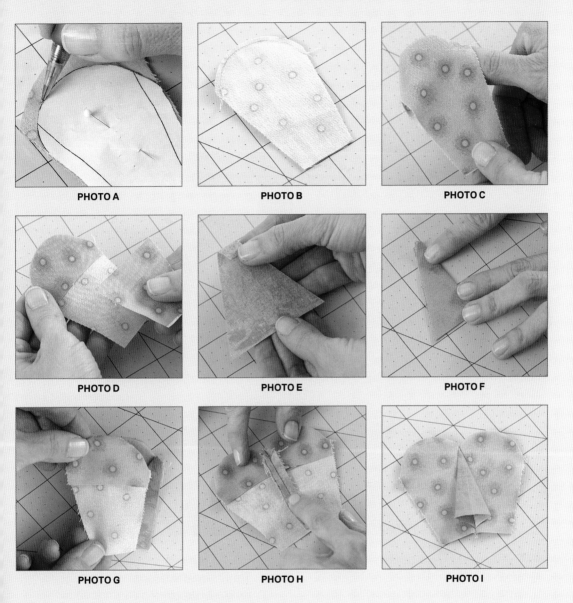

PHOTO A   PHOTO B   PHOTO C

PHOTO D   PHOTO E   PHOTO F

PHOTO G   PHOTO H   PHOTO I

dimensional folding technique

A. Mark seam line on half of raspberry batik A pieces.

B. Join two raspberry batik pieces along upper arcs; trim seam allowances to ⅛".

C. Turn joined A pieces right sides out to make a petal; press.

D. Trim one A piece ¼" from bottom edge of arc.

E. Fold tip of B triangle ¼" to wrong side.

F. Fold B triangle in half lengthwise.

G. Sandwich folded B triangle between two petals.

H. Sew all layers together, then finger-press seam open.

I. Press B triangle open to make a point. (When pressed open, lower edge of B triangle will be more than ¼" from bottom edge of petals.)

appliqué blocks

[1] With a glue stick, dab a small amount of glue on each petal tip of a sunburst appliqué. Position appliqué in center of a gold batik 12½" square and finger-press.

[2] Center a green batik C circle atop sunburst appliqué; glue or baste in place. Machine- or hand-stitch sunburst appliqué in place, starting with C circle.

Tip: To machine-appliqué, designer Edyta Sitar used clear monofilament thread in the needle and wound the bobbin with 100% cotton thread in a color to match the background fabric.

[3] Carefully cut a slit in gold batik under C circle and remove freezer paper to complete a block. Lightly press from wrong side.

[4] Repeat steps 1 through 3 to make three blocks total.

TABLE RUNNER ASSEMBLY DIAGRAM

finish table runner

[1] Sew together blocks and multicolor batik setting triangles in diagonal rows (**Table Runner Assembly Diagram**). Press seams toward setting triangles.

[2] Join rows to make table runner top; press seams in one direction.

[3] Layer table runner top, batting, and backing; baste. (For details, see Complete the Quilt, *page 159*.)

[4] Quilt as desired. This quilt features a stipple in the block backgrounds and a spiral in each C circle. A diagonal grid is stitched in the setting triangles.

[5] Bind with dark purple batik binding strips. (For details, see Complete the Quilt.)

faded rose

Stylized machine-appliqué roses done in soothing, soft colors look pretty on a chocolate brown background.

DESIGNER **CHERIE RALSTON**   MACHINE QUILTER **LORI KUKUK**   PHOTOGRAPHER **GREG SCHEIDEMANN**

materials

- 2⅝ yards dark brown dot (appliqué foundations, sashing)
- 4—9×22" pieces (fat eighths) in dusty pink, light brown, red, and gold prints (flower appliqués)
- ½ yard red plaid (flower appliqués, sashing squares)
- ¾ yard light green plaid (leaf and stem appliqués, binding)
- ⅓ yard light green stripe (leaf and stem appliqués)
- ½ yard light tan stripe (block borders)
- 3½ yards backing fabric
- 61" square batting
- Freezer paper
- Fabric glue stick

Finished quilt: 54½" square
Finished block: 16" square

Quantities are for 44/45"-wide, 100% cotton fabrics. **Measurements** include ¼" seam allowances. Sew with right sides together unless otherwise stated.

cut fabrics

Cut pieces in the following order. Patterns are on *Pattern Sheet 2*.

Designer Cherie Ralston uses a freezer-paper method to prepare pieces for machine appliqué. Instructions that follow are for this technique. (Patterns are provided for this technique; if you're using another method, reverse patterns using a light box or sunny window.)

[1] Lay freezer paper, shiny side down, over patterns. Trace each pattern the number of times indicated in cutting instructions. Cut out freezer-paper shapes on drawn lines.

[2] Using a hot, dry iron, press freezer-paper shapes, shiny sides down, onto designated fabrics' wrong sides, leaving ½" between shapes; let cool. Cut out each shape, adding a ³⁄₁₆" seam allowance to all edges. Cut seam allowances slightly narrower at tips of leaves and star points; clip inner curves as necessary.

[3] On each appliqué shape, run glue stick along wrong side of seam allowance, then fold seam allowance to back of freezer paper and finger-press; let dry.

From dark brown dot, cut:
▸ 4—18" squares
▸ 12—6½×18½" sashing rectangles

From dusty pink and light brown prints, cut:
▸ 4 each of patterns A, B, and K

From red plaid, cut:
▸ 9—6½" sashing squares

From red print and scraps of red plaid, cut:
▸ 4 each of patterns B, C, and L

From gold print, cut:
▸ 8 of Pattern D

From light green plaid, cut:
▸ Enough 2½"-wide bias strips to total 235" for binding (For details, see Cutting Bias Strips, *page 159.*)

From light green stripe and scraps of light green plaid, cut:
▸ 4 each of patterns E, F, G, I, and J
▸ 24 of Pattern H

From light tan stripe, cut:
▸ 8—1½×18½" strips
▸ 8—1½×16½" strips

appliqué blocks

[1] Fold each dark brown dot 18" square in half diagonally twice. Lightly press folds to create four foundation squares with appliqué placement guidelines; unfold.

[2] Referring to **Appliqué Placement Diagram**, lay out the following shapes on each brown dot foundation square and baste in place: one each of dusty pink or light brown print A, B, and K flowers; one each of red print or red plaid B, C, and L flowers; two gold print D flower centers; one each of light green stripe or plaid E, F, and G stems; six light green stripe or plaid H leaves; and one each of light green stripe or plaid I leaf and J flower.

[3] Using thread that matches the appliqué shades and working from bottom layer to top, machine-appliqué pieces to make four appliquéd blocks.

[4] Soak appliquéd blocks in cold water to remove glue. Machine-dry with dry towel to help absorb excess water. Trim foundation fabric behind appliqués, leaving ¼" seam allowances. Peel away freezer paper and discard. Press each block from wrong side and trim to 16½" square including seam allowances.

APPLIQUÉ PLACEMENT DIAGRAM

BLOCK ASSEMBLY DIAGRAM

assemble quilt top

[1] Sew light tan stripe 1½×16½" strips to opposite edges of an appliquéd block. Add light tan stripe 1½×18½" strips to remaining edges to make a bordered block (**Block Assembly Diagram**). Press all seams toward light tan strips.

[2] Repeat Step 1 to make four bordered blocks total.

[3] Referring to photo *(right)*, lay out dark brown dot sashing rectangles, red plaid sashing squares, and bordered blocks in five rows.

[4] Sew together pieces in each row. Press seams toward sashing rectangles in each row. Join rows to complete quilt top; press seams in one direction.

finish quilt

[1] Layer quilt top, batting, and backing; baste. (For details, see Complete the Quilt, *page 159*.)

[2] Quilt as desired. The featured quilt has machine-quilted details inside each appliqué shape, including loops in the stems, veins in the leaves, spirals in the flower centers, and circles and petal shapes in the flowers (**Quilting Diagram**). Each block background is echo-quilted around the appliqués with lines about ¼" apart. Feathered wreaths are stitched in each sashing square and a long line of feather quilting is stitched in each sashing rectangle.

[3] Bind with light green plaid binding strips. (For details, see Complete the Quilt.)

QUILTING DIAGRAM

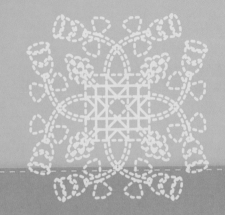

advanced

Challenge yourself with a trio of appliqué
projects filled with interesting details and
hand-stitched embellishments.

butterfly
garden

Use an overlay method of appliqué to assure the accurate placement of each butterfly and flower on this wall-hanging-size quilt.

DESIGNERS **BECKY GOLDSMITH** AND **LINDA JENKINS**
PHOTOGRAPHER **PERRY STRUSE**

materials

- 1⅞ yards of muslin for appliqué foundations and inner border
- Scraps of assorted purple, yellow, green, pink, red, blue, orange, and tan for appliqués
- ⅓ yard of green pin dot for appliqués and inner border
- ⅓ yard of green stripe for appliqués
- ⅓ yard of green polka dot for binding
- 41" square of backing fabric
- 41" square of quilt batting
- Embroidery floss in colors to match the appliqués
- ¼ yard of clear upholstery vinyl or other clear flexible plastic (optional)

Finished quilt top: 35" square
Finished block: 5" square

Quantities specified for 44/45"-wide, 100% cotton fabrics. **Measurements** include a ¼" seam allowance. Sew with right sides together unless otherwise indicated.

designer notes

Project designers Becky Goldsmith and Linda Jenkins have developed their own appliqué method, which uses an overlay for placement purposes. The following instructions are for their overlay method. (For more information, see Overlay Method on *page 24.*) Your favorite appliqué method also can be used.

They advise pairing fabrics before cutting to make sure you have enough coordinating prints.

make appliqué templates

[1] The patterns are on *Pattern Sheet* 4. Trace pattern pieces 1 through 14 onto template plastic.

[2] Cut out the templates on the drawn lines with sharp scissors. Keep the template edges smooth and points sharp.

[3] Mark the right side of each template with the proper number. The numbers indicate the appliquéing sequence.

cut fabrics

To make the best use of your fabrics, cut the pieces in the order that follows. The appliqué foundations are cut larger than necessary to allow for sewing differences. You'll trim the foundations to the correct size after completing the appliqué. When cutting out the appliqué pieces, lay the fabrics and template with right sides up; trace. Add a ³⁄₁₆" seam allowance to all edges when cutting out the appliqué pieces. Cut the border strips the length of the fabric (parallel to the selvage). The border strip measurements are mathematically correct. You may wish to cut your border strips longer than specified to allow for possible sewing differences.

From muslin, cut:
- 4—7×27" rectangles for border appliqué foundations
- 4—1³⁄₄×40" strips for inner border
- 20—7" squares for appliqué foundations

From assorted purple, yellow, and green print scraps, cut:
- 6 each of patterns 1, 2, 3, and 4

From assorted pink and red print scraps, cut:
- 20 of Pattern 14
- 6 each of patterns 1, 2, 3, and 4

From assorted blue print scraps, cut:
- 28 of Pattern 7
- 3 each of patterns 1, 2, 3, and 4

From assorted orange print scraps, cut:
- 1 each of patterns 1, 2, 3, and 4
- 4 of Pattern 8

From assorted tan print scraps, cut:
- 16 of Pattern 5

From green pin dot, cut:
- 4—1³⁄₄×40" strips for inner border
- 4 of Pattern 6
- 20 of Pattern 11

From green stripe, cut:
- 20 each of patterns 12 and 13
- 4 each of patterns 9 and 10

From green polka dot, cut:
- 4—2½×40" binding strips

From upholstery vinyl, cut:
- 3—5" squares

appliqué blocks and outer border

[1] Lightly press the muslin 7" squares in half horizontally and vertically to form placement lines; unfold.

[2] Position a vinyl 5" square over the **Butterfly Appliqué Placement Diagram** on *Pattern Sheet 4*, and accurately trace the design once, including the dashed placement lines, with a permanent marker.

[3] Position the overlay on a creased muslin 7" foundation square, orienting the overlay's placement lines with the pressed lines. Pin the top of the overlay to the fabric, if desired.

[4] Slide a Pattern 1 wing piece, right side up, between the foundation square and the overlay. Be sure to leave enough fabric at one end so pattern pieces 3 and 5 can cover it. When the wing piece is in place, remove the overlay, pin the wing to the foundation, and appliqué it in place.

[5] Use the overlay to position the next piece in the stitching sequence. Working in numerical order, continue in this manner—positioning the pieces right side up under the overlay, removing the overlay to pin them to the background, and appliquéing them in place—until a butterfly block is completed.

[6] Backstitch the butterfly antennae using one strand of floss and tiny stitches. Becky and Linda matched the floss color to the color of the butterfly's wings.

[7] Press the appliquéd butterfly block from the back; trim it to measure 5½" square, including the seam allowances.

[8] Repeat steps 3 through 7 to make a total of 16 appliquéd butterfly blocks.

[9] Repeat steps 2 through 5, tracing the **Daisy Appliqué Placement Diagram** on *Pattern Sheet* 4, to make a total of four appliquéd daisy blocks. Press the appliquéd daisy blocks. Trim each one to measure 5¾" square, including the seam allowances.

[10] Lightly press a muslin 7×27" rectangle in half horizontally and vertically to form placement lines. Press two additional vertical placement lines on either side of the center crease, evenly spacing them 4¾" apart, to make a total of five vertical placement lines. Lightly press the same placement lines in the remaining three muslin 7×27" rectangles.

[11] Referring to the photograph above right for placement, repeat steps 2 through 5, tracing the **Tulip Appliqué Placement Diagram** on *Pattern Sheet 4*, to appliqué five tulips on each creased muslin 7×27" foundation rectangle. Press the appliquéd tulip rectangles. Trim each to measure 5½×25½", including the seam allowances, to make a total of four appliquéd tulip border strips.

assemble quilt center

[1] Referring to the photograph for placement, lay out the butterfly blocks in four horizontal rows. Sew together the blocks in each row. Press the seam allowances in one direction, alternating the direction with each row.

[2] Join the rows to make the quilt center. Press the seam allowances in one direction. The pieced quilt center should measure 20½" square, including the seam allowances.

assemble and add inner border

[1] Aligning long edges, sew together one green pin-dot 1¾×40" strip and one muslin 1¾×40" strip to make a strip set (see **Diagram 1**). Press the seam allowance toward the green pin dot strip. Repeat to make a total of four strip sets.

[2] Cut the strip sets into a total of seventy-two 1¾"-wide segments.

[3] Join sixteen 1¾"-wide segments in a row to make a checkerboard border strip (see **Diagram 2**). The pieced checkerboard border strip should measure 3×20½", including the seam allowances. Repeat to make a second checkerboard border strip of the same size. Sew the checkerboard border strips to opposite edges of the pieced quilt center. Press the seam allowances toward the checkerboard border.

[4] Sew together twenty 1¾"-wide segments to make a checkerboard border strip that measures 3×25½", including the seam allowances. Repeat to make second checkerboard border strip of the same size. Sew these checkerboard border strips to the remaining edges of the pieced quilt center. Press the seam allowances toward the checkerboard border.

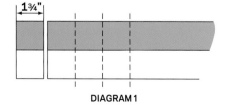

1¾"

DIAGRAM 1

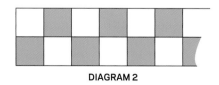

DIAGRAM 2

add outer border

[1] Referring to the photograph on *page 139*, sew an appliquéd tulip border strip to opposite edges of the pieced quilt center. Press the seam allowances toward the appliquéd border.

[2] Sew an appliquéd daisy block to each end of the remaining appliquéd tulip border strips to make two border units. Sew the border units to the remaining edges of the pieced quilt center to complete the quilt top. Press the seam allowances toward the appliquéd border.

finish quilt

[1] Layer the quilt top, batting, and backing. (For details, see Complete the Quilt, *page 159*.)

[2] Quilt as desired. This quilt was echo-quilted with butterfly, tulip, and daisy appliqués. To add contrast to the many curves in the quilt, an X was machine-

quilted on each muslin square in the checkerboard border.

[3] Bind with green polka-dot binding strips. (For details, see Complete the Quilt.)

optional sizes

ALTERNATE QUILT SIZES	TWIN	FULL/QUEEN	KING
Number of blocks	126	224	324
Number of blocks wide by long	9×14	14×16	18×18
Finished size	60×85"	85×95"	105" square
YARDAGE REQUIREMENTS			
Muslin—borders cut the length of fabric	7½ yards	10½ yards	13⅞ yards
Assorted fabrics for appliqués	3 yards	5½ yards	9 yards
Green pin dot	¾ yard	⅞ yard	1 yard
Green stripe for appliqués	1 yard	2 yards	2⅞ yards
Binding	⅝ yard	⅔ yard	⅞ yard
Backing	5⅛ yards	7⅝ yards	9¼ yards
Batting	66×91"	91×101"	111" square

berries&buds

Patchwork stars and lavish machine appliqué adorn this intricate and heirloom-worthy quilt.

DESIGNER **KIM DIEHL**   MACHINE QUILTER **CELESTE FREIBERG**   PHOTOGRAPHER **PETE KRUMHARDT**

materials

- ▸ 9—9×22" pieces (fat eighths) assorted red prints (blocks, bud appliqués, borders, binding)
- ▸ 2¾ yards tan print (blocks)
- ▸ 1 yard mottled green (vine appliqués)
- ▸ 2 yards total assorted red prints (bud appliqués, borders, binding)
- ▸ 2¾ yards tan tone-on-tone print (borders)
- ▸ ⅞ yard total assorted green prints (leaf appliqués)
- ▸ ½ yard total assorted gold prints (calyx appliqués)
- ▸ 1¼ yards total assorted purple prints (berry appliqués)
- ▸ 4½ yards backing fabric
- ▸ 79×81" batting
- ▸ Freezer paper (optional)
- ▸ Monofilament thread (optional)
- ▸ No. 8 perle cotton: black
- ▸ No. 5 embroidery needle
- ▸ Liquid fabric basting glue

Finished quilt: 72½×74½"
Finished block: 18" square

Quantities are for 44/45"-wide, 100% cotton fabrics. **Measurements** include ¼" seam allowances. Sew with right sides together unless otherwise stated.

cut fabrics

Cut pieces in the order that follows. Cut border strips lengthwise (parallel to selvage).

From *each* of nine assorted red print fat eighths, cut:
- ▸ 1—2½" square
- ▸ 4—1½×2½" rectangles
- ▸ 12—1½" squares

From tan print, cut:
- ▸ 18—6½×18½" rectangles
- ▸ 18—6½" squares
- ▸ 72—1½×2½" rectangles
- ▸ 144—1½" squares

From mottled green, cut:
- ▸ Enough 1¼"-wide bias strips to total 880" in length for vine and stem appliqués (For details, see Cutting Bias Strips, *page 159*.)

From remaining red print fat eighths and assorted red prints, cut:
- ▸ Enough 2½"-wide strips in lengths varying from 6" to 36" to total 330" in length for binding
- ▸ 4—1⅞" squares
- ▸ 532—1½" squares

From tan tone-on-tone print, cut:
- 2—7½×72½" middle border strips
- 2—8½×56½" middle border strips
- 246—1½×2½" rectangles
- 4—1⅞" squares
- 4—1½" squares

piece foundation blocks

[1] For one foundation block, you'll need one red print 2½" square, four matching red print 1½×2½" rectangles, 12 matching red print 1½" squares, four assorted red print 1½" squares, eight tan print 1½×2½" rectangles, 16 tan print 1½" squares, two tan print 6½×18½" rectangles, and two tan print 6½" squares.

[2] Mark a diagonal line on the wrong side of eight matching red print 1½" squares, four assorted red print 1½" squares, and 12 tan print 1½" squares.

[3] Align marked tan print 1½" squares with opposite corners of a red print 2½" square (**Diagram 1**; note placement of marked lines). Sew on marked lines; trim excess, leaving a ¼" seam allowance. Press attached triangles open.

[4] Align and sew marked tan print 1½" squares to remaining corners of red print 2½" square (**Diagram 2**).

Trim and press as before to make a Square-in-a-Square unit. The Square-in-a-Square unit should be 2½" square including seam allowances.

[5] Align a marked tan print 1½" square with one end of a red print 1½×2½" rectangle (**Diagram 3**; note placement of marked line). Sew on marked line; trim excess, leaving a ¼" seam allowance. Press attached triangle open.

[6] Align and sew a second marked tan print 1½" square to opposite end of red print 1½×2½" rectangle (**Diagram 3**; note placement of marked line). Trim and press as before to make a red print Flying Geese unit. The red print Flying Geese unit should still be 1½×2½" including seam allowances.

[7] Repeat steps 5 and 6 to make four red print Flying Geese units total.

[8] Repeat steps 5 and 6 using tan print 1½×2½" rectangles and red print 1½" squares to make four tan print Flying Geese units total (**Diagram 4**).

[9] Lay out a Square-in-a-Square unit, four red print Flying Geese units, and four red print 1½" squares in rows (**Diagram 5**). Sew together pieces in each row. Press seams toward red print squares or Square-in-a-Square unit. Join rows to

tip

"The small scale of many of these appliqué pieces lends itself to a smaller machine stitch," Kim says. "Use a tiny zigzag stitch to make your appliqués more secure and the stitches less visible, and to create fewer gaps between tacking stitches."

make a center unit. Press seams toward center row. The center unit should be 4½" square including seam allowances.

[10] Lay out four tan print 1½" squares and two tan print Flying Geese units in rows (Diagram 6). Sew together pieces in each row. Press seams toward tan print squares. Join rows to opposite edges of center unit. Press seams toward added rows.

[11] Lay out four tan print 1½×2½" rectangles and two tan print Flying Geese units in rows (Diagram 7). Sew together pieces in each row. Press seams toward tan print rectangles. Join rows to remaining edges of center unit to make a star unit. Press seams toward added rows. The star unit should be 6½" square including seam allowances.

[12] Lay out two tan print 6½×18½" rectangles, two tan print 6½" squares, and star unit in rows (Diagram 8). Sew together pieces in center row. Press seams toward tan print squares. Join rows to make a block unit. Press seams toward tan print rectangles. The block unit should be 18½" square including seam allowances.

[13] Sew marked assorted red print 1½" squares to each corner of block unit (Diagram 9; note placement of marked lines). Trim excess, leaving ¼" seam allowances. Press attached triangles open to make a foundation block. The foundation block should be 18½" square including seam allowances.

[14] Repeat steps 1 through 13 to make nine foundation blocks total.

DIAGRAM 1   DIAGRAM 2

DIAGRAM 3   DIAGRAM 4

DIAGRAM 5   DIAGRAM 6   DIAGRAM 7

DIAGRAM 8

DIAGRAM 9

prepare appliqués

Kim uses a freezer-paper method for appliquéing. The following instructions are for this technique. Patterns are on *Pattern Sheet 1*.

[1] Trace patterns onto dull side of freezer paper, leaving at least ¼" between tracings. Cut out freezer-paper templates on traced lines.

[2] Place a small amount of fabric glue on dull side of freezer-paper shapes and position them on wrong side of designated fabrics, leaving ½" between pieces A, B, C, and D. **Note:** Pattern E does not need seam allowances. To save time, position freezer-paper template E over multiple layers of fabric and cut out several fabric shapes at once.

[3] Cut out A, B, C, and D fabric shapes, adding ¼" seam allowances. Clip curves. Cut out E fabric shapes on traced lines.

From assorted green prints, cut:
▸ 208 of Pattern D
From remaining red print fat eighths and assorted red prints, cut:
▸ 84 each of patterns A and B

From assorted gold prints, cut:
▸ 84 of Pattern C
From assorted purple prints, cut:
▸ 400 of Pattern E

[4] On appliqués A, B, C, and D, use the tip of a hot, dry iron to fold the seam allowance over the edge of the freezer paper. Continue working around the appliqué shape, folding over one area at a time and pressing the seam allowance up and over the freezer paper. Remove freezer paper from E appliqués.

[5] Piece mottled green 1¼"-wide bias strips into an 880"-long strip.

[6] Fold mottled green 880"-long bias strip in half lengthwise with the wrong side inside; press. Stitching a scant ¼" from the edges, sew together long edges (**Diagram 10**, *page 147*). Trim seam allowance to ⅛". Refold strip, centering seam in back; press.

[7] Cut prepared mottled green strip into:
▸ 2—38"-long vine appliqués
▸ 4—28"-long vine appliqués
▸ 72—7½"-long stem appliqués
▸ 10—3"-long stem appliqués
▸ 40—2½"-long stem appliqués

[8] Turn under a ¼" seam allowance on one end of each mottled green 7½"-long and 2½"-long stem appliqué; secure with a dab of fabric glue.

[9] Using a knotted length of black perle cotton, a No. 5 embroidery needle, and a running stitch, sew around a purple print E circle ⅛" from outer raw edge without turning seam under (**Diagram 11**); do not cut thread. Gently pull thread tails to gather edge into the center to make a yo-yo; knot and clip thread. Press yo-yo flat from the gathered side to form a berry appliqué. Repeat to make 400 berry appliqués total.

appliqué blocks

[1] Position eight mottled green 7½"-long stem appliqués and four mottled green 2½"-long stem appliqués on a

foundation block with the turned-under end of each stem abutting the star unit; baste in place (**Stem Appliqué Placement Diagram**).

[**2**] Working from bottom to top, use monofilament thread to machine-blindstitch or zigzag-stitch stems in place. The distance between each zigzag should be ⅛" maximum, and the width of the zigzag should be the width of two or three threads. You should be able to see needle holes, but no thread. If you gently pull on the edge of the appliqué, stitching should be strong with no gaps. **Note:** If your stitching shows, you may be stitching too far from the edge of the appliqué. If you miss stitching into the appliqué with the zigzag, stitches will be visible. Gaps indicate stitch length may be too long. If you see too much of the zigzag stitch, it is too wide.

[**3**] Lay out eight red print A buds, eight red print B bud centers, eight gold print C calyxes, 16 green print D leaves, and 32 purple print E berries on foundation block; baste in place (**Block Appliqué Placement Diagram**). **Note:** Kim suggests placing a small dot of liquid fabric glue on the gathered side of each yo-yo and pressing it onto foundation to eliminate the need for pins.

[**4**] Working from bottom to top, use monofilament thread to machine-blindstitch or zigzag-stitch pieces in place. **Note:** If you are appliquéing by hand, leave a ½" opening along each piece and remove freezer-paper shapes; if you are appliquéing by machine, this opening is not needed (see Step 5).

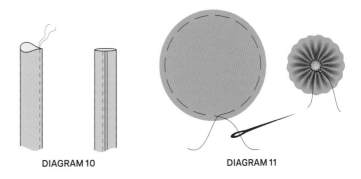

DIAGRAM 10   DIAGRAM 11

STEM APPLIQUÉ PLACEMENT DIAGRAM

BLOCK APPLIQUÉ PLACEMENT DIAGRAM

[5] On the back side of each appliquéd A, B, C, and D piece, trim excess foundation block, leaving a ¼" seam allowance. With your fingertip or the tip of your needle, gently peel freezer paper away from fabric.

[6] Repeat steps 1 through 5 to appliqué nine blocks total.

assemble quilt center

[1] Lay out appliquéd blocks in rows (Quilt Assembly Diagram).

[2] Sew together blocks in each row. Press seams in one direction, alternating direction with each row. Join rows to make quilt center. Press seams in one direction. The quilt center should be 54½" square including seam allowances.

assemble and add borders

[1] Mark a diagonal line on the wrong side of 492 red print 1½" squares and four red print 1⅞" squares.

[2] Using marked red print 1½" squares and tan tone-on-tone print 1½×2½" rectangles, repeat Piece Foundation Blocks, page 144, steps 5 and 6, to make 246 tan tone-on-tone print Flying Geese units.

[3] Sew together 27 tan tone-on-tone print Flying Geese units to make an inner border unit (Quilt Assembly Diagram). Press seams in one direction. The inner border unit should be 54½" long including seam allowances. Repeat to make four inner border units total.

[4] Sew inner border units to opposite edges of quilt center. Press seams toward quilt center.

[5] Sew a tan tone-on-tone print 1½" square to each end of remaining inner border units. Press seams toward tan squares. Join pieced inner border units to remaining edges of quilt center. Press seams toward quilt center. The quilt center should be 56½" square including seam allowances.

[6] Sew a tan tone-on-tone print 8½×56½" middle border strip to opposite edges of quilt center. Join tan tone-on-tone print 7½×72½" middle border strips to remaining edges. Press all seams toward middle border. The quilt center should be 70½×72½" including seam allowances.

[7] Sew together 35 tan tone-on-tone print Flying Geese units to make a long outer border unit (Quilt Assembly Diagram). Press seams in one direction. The long outer border unit should be 70½" long including seam allowances. Repeat to make a second long outer border unit.

[8] Sew together 34 tan tone-on-tone print Flying Geese units to make a short outer border unit (Quilt Assembly Diagram). Press seams in one direction. The short outer border unit should be 68½" long including seam allowances. Repeat to make a second short outer border unit.

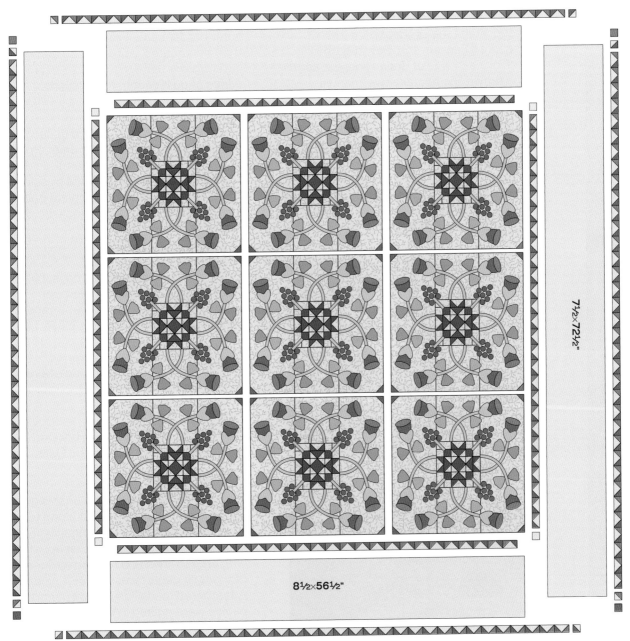

7½×72½"

8½×56½"

QUILT ASSEMBLY DIAGRAM

[9] Layer a marked red print 1⅞" square atop a tan tone-on-tone print 1⅞" square (**Diagram 12**). Sew together ¼" on each side of drawn line; cut apart on drawn line to make two triangle units. Press each triangle unit open to make a triangle-square. Each triangle-square should be 1½" square including seam allowances. Repeat to make eight triangle-squares total.

DIAGRAM 12

[10] Sew a triangle-square to each end of outer border units. Press seams toward triangle-squares. Join short pieced outer border units to top and bottom edges of quilt center. Press seams toward middle border.

[11] Sew a red print 1½" square to each end of the long outer border units. Press seams toward red print squares. Join pieced long outer border units to side edges of quilt center to complete quilt top. Press seams toward middle border.

appliqué border

[1] Referring to photograph on *page 151*, place remaining appliqué pieces on opposite corners of tan tone-on-tone print middle border; baste in place.

[2] Repeat Appliqué Blocks, *page 146*, steps 4 and 5, to appliqué middle border.

finish quilt

[1] Layer quilt top, batting, and backing. (For details, see Complete the Quilt, *page 159*.)

[2] Quilt as desired. Each berry on this quilt was outlined with machine quilting to emphasize the shape and enhance its raised appearance. The stars were quilted with arched lines and the background of the quilt center was micro-stippled. A feathered medallion and serpentine cables were quilted in the open border corners and the border background was filled with a pebble-like motif.

[3] Use assorted red print binding strips to bind quilt. (For details, see Complete the Quilt)

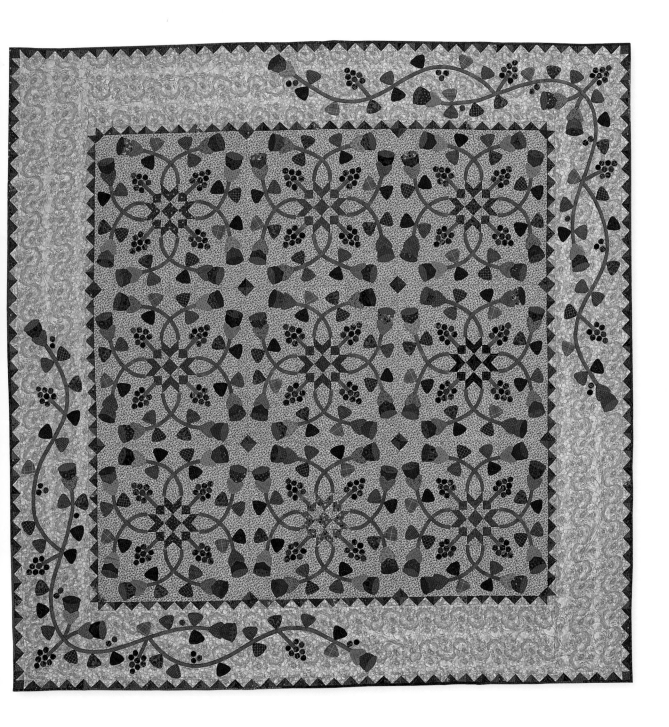

Rustic details, such as utility stitching and intentionally visible knots, make this small quilt a gardener's delight.

DESIGNER **TONEE WHITE** PHOTOGRAPHERS **GREG SCHEIDEMANN** AND **MARTY BALDWIN**

materials

- ½ yard muslin (appliqué foundation)
- ¼ yard solid light olive green (letter appliqués)
- 5" square each of solid brown and solid light brown (pot appliqués)
- 9×22" piece (fat eighth) solid dark green (stem appliqués)
- ¼ yard dark olive green print (leaf appliqués)
- ½ yard backing fabric
- 15×31" batting
- Perle cotton No. 8: olive green

Finished quilt: 15×31"

Quantities are for 44/45"-wide, 100% cotton fabrics. **Measurements** include ¼" seam allowances unless otherwise specified. Sew with right sides together unless otherwise stated.

cut fabrics

Cut pieces in the following order. Patterns are on *Pattern Sheet 4*. To make templates of the patterns, see Make and Use Templates, *page 157*.

To use designer Tonee White's needle-turn method for appliquéing, complete the following steps to prepare appliqué pieces.

[1] With fabric right side up, position each template faceup on fabrics specified in cutting instructions. Use a pencil or a fine-line permanent marker to trace each pattern the number of times indicated, leaving at least ½" between tracings.

[2] Cut out each fabric shape a scant ¼" outside drawn lines.

From muslin, cut:
- 1—16×32" rectangle

From solid light olive green, cut:
- 1 of letter D
- 2 each of letters S and E

From solid brown, cut:
- 1 of Pattern B

From solid light brown, cut:
- 1 of Pattern A

From solid dark green, cut:
- Enough ½"-wide bias strips to total 72" for stems (For details, see Cutting Bias Strips, *page 159*.)

From dark olive green print, cut:
- 185 of Pattern C

From backing fabric, cut:
- 1—16×32" rectangle

the appliquilt technique

Tonee has developed a one-step method of appliquéing and quilting called Appliquilt, in which she adds appliqués to a quilt top that is already layered with the batting and backing. All layers are sewn through when adding the appliqués. The instructions that follow are for this method.

prepare appliqué foundation

[1] Using a clear acrylic ruler and a pencil, lightly draw a rectangle 1¼" from raw edges of muslin 16×32" rectangle. Draw four more rectangles every ½" inside first rectangle (**Marking Diagram**).

[2] Center marked muslin rectangle atop batting and backing rectangles; baste.

[3] Using olive green perle cotton and a running stitch, sew through all layers on drawn lines. To duplicate the utility

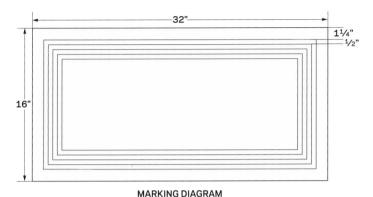

MARKING DIAGRAM

RUNNING STITCH

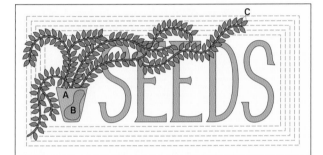

APPLIQUÉ PLACEMENT DIAGRAM

OVERCAST STITCH

stitch that Tonee used, begin stitching from the top, leaving a 6" thread tail. When ending thread, leave a 6" thread tail on the quilt top. Begin the next thread about ⅛" away from the end thread tail; after a few stitches, tie thread tails together and clip ends to ¼" (Running Stitch Diagram).

appliqué quilt top

[1] Position solid light olive green letters on quilted muslin rectangle; baste (Appliqué Placement Diagram). (To add a primitive look to her wall hanging, Tonee positioned her first S upside down.)

[2] Thread your needle with olive green perle cotton. Using drawn line as a guide, turn under seam allowance of each letter with your needle and use an overcast stitch to hand-sew through all layers (Overcast Stitch Diagram). Along curves, make small clips into seam allowance to turn it under.

To make an overcast stitch, bring your needle up about ⅛" to 1/16" inside the appliqué edge (A on Overcast Stitch Diagram). Insert needle back into appliqué foundation at B, just outside the edge of the appliqué, and bring it up at C. Continue in same manner around shape.

[3] Using matching thread and an overcast stitch, hand-sew the solid brown B shadow piece to the solid light brown A flowerpot. Appliqué both pieces to quilted muslin rectangle, leaving top of flowerpot open to insert stems.

[4] Referring to photo on *pages 152–153* and **Appliqué Placement Diagram** on *page 155*, position solid dark green stems on quilted muslin rectangle. Using matching thread and an overcast stitch, hand-appliqué in place through all layers, turning edges of each stem under $\frac{3}{16}$" as you stitch. Once all stems are stitched in place, hand-sew top of flowerpot closed.

[5] Arrange dark olive green print C leaves along edges of each stem; pin or baste. Using matching thread and an overcast stitch, hand-appliqué each piece in place, sewing through all quilt layers.

finish quilt

[1] Fold edges of muslin background $\frac{1}{2}$" over batting on all sides and pin in place.

[2] Fold under backing $\frac{1}{2}$" on all sides so that folded edge is even with folded edge of muslin background. Using thread to match muslin background, whipstitch edges of the piece closed to complete the quilt.

quilting
basics

Refer to these tips and techniques whenever you need information for your projects.

make and use templates

When making templates, use easy-to-cut transparent template plastic, available at crafts supply stores.

To make a template, lay the plastic over a printed pattern. Trace the pattern using a permanent marker (and ruler for straight lines). Mark template with project name, letter, and any marked matching points (**Photo 1**).

For machine piecing, the solid lines are cutting lines, and dashed lines are seam lines. (An arrow on a pattern indicates the direction the fabric grain should run.)

Cut out the template and check it against the original pattern for accuracy (**Photo 2**). Any error (even if small) will multiply as you assemble the project.

Using a pushpin, make a hole in the template at all marked matching points (**Photo 3**). The hole must be large enough to accommodate a pencil point.

To trace the template on fabric, use a pencil, a dressmaker's white pencil, chalk, or a special fabric marker that makes a thin, accurate line. Don't use a ballpoint or ink pen, which may bleed. Test all marking tools on a fabric scrap before using them. Place your fabric right side down on 220-grit sandpaper to prevent the fabric from stretching as you trace. Place the template facedown on the wrong side of the fabric with the template's grain line parallel to the fabric's lengthwise or crosswise grain. Trace around the template. Mark any matching points through the

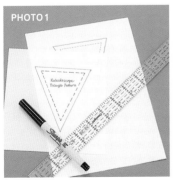

PHOTO 1

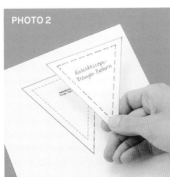

PHOTO 2

PHOTO 3

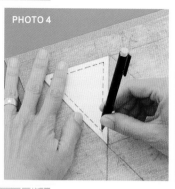

PHOTO 4

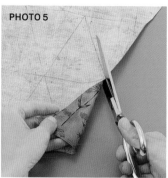

PHOTO 5

holes in the template (**Photo 4**). (When sewing pieces together, line up and pin through matching points to ensure accurate assembly.)

Repeat to trace the number of pieces needed, positioning the tracings without space between them. Use shears or scissors (or a rotary cutter and ruler) to precisely cut fabric pieces on the drawn lines (**Photo 5**).

For appliqué and hand piecing, the dashed lines indicate finished size; add needed seam allowance as instructed in project.

piece and appliqué

stitching: Quilting depends upon accuracy at every step. Use exact ¼" seam allowances throughout a quilt's construction. It isn't necessary to backstitch at the beginning of any seam that will be intersected by another seam later in the quiltmaking process. Use a stitch length of 10–12 stitches per inch (2.0- to 2.5-mm setting) to prevent stitches from unraveling before they're stitched over again. Secure seams that won't be sewn across again (such as those in borders) with a few backstitches.

pinning: When you want seams to line up perfectly, match up seams of pieced units, and then place an extra-fine pin diagonally through the pieces, catching both seam allowances. Avoid sewing over pins because this can damage your machine and injure you.

pressing: Pressing seams ensures accurate piecing. Set the seam first by pressing it as it was sewn, without opening the fabric pieces. This helps sink the stitches into the fabric, leaving you with a less bulky seam allowance.

The direction you press the seam allowance is important and is usually specified in the instructions. Typically you will press the entire seam to one side rather than open. When two seams will be joined, press the seams in opposite directions; this helps line up the seams perfectly and reduces bulk.

Make sure you are pressing, not ironing. Ironing means moving the iron while it is in contact with the fabric; this stretches and distorts seams. Pressing involves lifting the iron off the surface of the fabric and putting it back down in another location.

CUTTING ON THE BIAS

Bias runs diagonally between the lengthwise and crosswise grain lines of a woven fabric. The true bias runs exactly at a 45° angle to the grain lines (**Diagram 1**) and has the most stretch in a woven fabric.

Because of their built-in stretch, strips cut on the bias can be easily curved or shaped. Use them when binding curved edges or to make curved appliqué pieces such as vines or stems.

You can also cut directional fabrics such as plaids or stripes on the bias for purely visual reasons. A bias binding cut from a striped fabric creates a "barber pole" effect.

cutting bias strips: To cut bias strips, begin with a fabric square or rectangle. Using an acrylic ruler and a rotary cutter, cut one edge at a 45° angle. Measure the desired width from the cut edge and then make a cut parallel to the edge (Photo 6). Repeat until you have the desired number of strips. Handle bias strips carefully to avoid distorting the fabric.

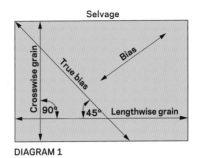

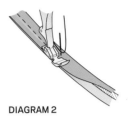

DIAGRAM 1 **DIAGRAM 2**

covered cording

Covered cording is made by sewing a bias-cut fabric strip around a length of cording. The width of the bias strip will vary depending on the diameter of your cording. Refer to the specific project instructions for those measurements. Regardless, the method used to cover the cording is the same.

With the wrong side inside, fold under 1½" at one end of the bias strip. With wrong side inside, fold the strip in half lengthwise to make the cording cover. Insert the cording next to the folded edge, placing a cording end 1" from the cording cover folded end. Using a machine cording foot, sew through both fabric layers right next to the cording (Diagram 2).

When attaching the cording to your project, begin stitching 1½" from the covered cording's folded end.

After going around the entire edge of the project, cut the end of the cording so that it will fit snugly into the folded opening at the beginning. The ends of the cording should abut inside the covering. Stitch the ends in place to secure.

complete the quilt

assemble the layers: Cut and piece the backing fabric to measure at least 3" bigger than the quilt top on all sides. Press seams open. Place the quilt backing wrong side up on a flat surface. Center and smooth the batting atop the quilt backing. Center the quilt top right side up on top of the batting and smooth out any wrinkles. Use safety pins or long hand stitches to baste the layers together.

quilt as desired: A few of the more common machine-quilting methods follow.

Stitching in the ditch. Stitch just inside a seam line; the stitches should almost disappear into the seam. Using a walking foot attachment on your sewing machine will help prevent the quilt layers from shifting.

Stipple quilting. This random, allover stitching provides texture and interest behind a pattern. Use a darning foot and lower the feed dogs on your machine.

Outline quilting. Stitch ¼" from a seam line or the edge of an appliqué shape, just past the extra thickness of the seam allowance.

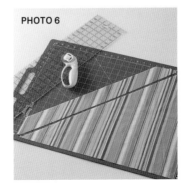

PHOTO 6

trim quilt: Trim the batting and backing fabric even with the quilt top edges; machine-baste a scant ¼" from quilt top edges if desired. (Some quilters prefer to wait until they have machine-sewn the binding to the quilt top before trimming the batting and backing.)

BETTER BINDING

cut the strips: The cutting instructions for each project tell you the width and number of binding strips to cut. Unless otherwise specified, cut binding strips on the straight grain of the fabric. Join the binding strips with diagonal seams to make one long binding strip (**Photo 7**). Trim seams to ¼" and press open.

attach the binding: With the wrong side inside, fold under 1" at one end of the binding strip and press. Then fold the strip in half lengthwise with the wrong side inside. Place the binding strip against the right side of the quilt top along one edge, aligning the binding strip's raw edges with the quilt top's raw edge (do not start at a corner). Begin sewing the binding in place 2" from the folded end.

turn the corner: Stop sewing when you're ¼" from the corner (or a distance equal to the seam allowance you're using).

Backstitch; then clip the threads (**Photo 8**). Remove the quilt from under the sewing-machine presser foot.

Fold the binding strip upward, creating a diagonal fold, and finger-press (**Photo 9**).

Holding the diagonal fold in place with your finger, bring the binding strip down in line with the next edge, making a horizontal fold that aligns with the quilt edge. Start sewing again at the top of the horizontal fold, stitching through all layers (**Photo 10**). Sew around the quilt, turning each corner in the same manner.

finish it: When you return to the starting point, encase the binding strip's raw edge inside the folded end and finish sewing to the starting point. Trim the batting and backing fabric even with the quilt top edges if not done earlier.

Turn the binding over the edge to the back. Hand-stitch the binding to the backing fabric only, covering any machine stitching. To make the binding corners on the quilt back match the mitered corners on the quilt front, hand-stitch up to a corner and make a fold in the binding. Secure the fold with a couple stitches; then continue stitching the binding in place along the next edge.

PHOTO 7

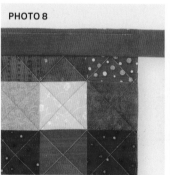
PHOTO 8

PHOTO 9

PHOTO 10